Affirmations
of a
Skeptical Believer

Affirmations
of a
Skeptical
Believer

by

G. Avery Lee

 Mercer
University Press

ISBN 0-86554-395-X

Affirmations
of a Skeptical Believer
Copyright © 1991
Mercer University Press
Macon GA 31207
All rights reserved
Printed in the United States of America

Library of Congress Cataloging-in-Publication Data
Lee, G. Avery, 1916–
    Affirmations of a skeptical believer /
by G. Avery Lee.
    xii + 125 pp., 6 × 9″ (15 × 23cm).
    Includes bibliographical references.
    ISBN 0-86554-395-X
    1. Apologetics—20th century.   I. Title.
BT1102.L43   1991   91-15440
239—dc20   CIP

CONTENTS

†   Preface   ix

†   An Agnostic Can Be a Christian   1

†   God Is   9

†   Who and What Is Man?   27

†   Sin? What's That?   39

†   A View of the Bible   53

†   Looking at Jesus Christ   71

†   The Second Most Beautiful Words   85

†   The Necessity of a Sense of Humor   97

† What about Miracles?   109

† A Christian Quest through Faith,
Doubt, and the Church   117

† This Life, Then Death:
Is that All There Is?   137

† A Sermon
"The Impossible Dream"   153

To
Natasha Ann LaCoste
(granddaughter)

'Tash,

Question the branches, not the Tree,
Disbelieve lesser gods in favor of God.
Trust without professing to know it all.
Believe where you cannot prove.
Be confident in hope,
Even if you can't always see.
Find your own Affirmations.
May they be meaningful,
As mine have been.

✝ *Hear, O Israel:*
the Lord our God is one Lord.
—Deuteronomy 6:4
The Shema, watchword of Jewish monotheism

I believe; help my unbelief! —Mark 9:24

Never give up the search for knowledge and
truth.
—final admonition
from Professor W. D. Bond in a course
in Modern British and American Poetry,
Hardin-Simmons University,
Abilene, Texas, 28 May 1938

My religious faith remains in possession of
the field only after prolonged civil war with
my naturally skeptical mind.
—William Lyon Phelps

† PREFACE

Shortly after I announced my second retirement, a friend asked how I perceived the Christian faith now that I was in the twilight years.

"Well," I said, "I don't believe as much as I once did. . . . But what I do believe, I believe more firmly."

This credo has been hammered out on a personal anvil, with the help of some friends, and an occasional adversary. We begin life with a new anvil. An unused anvil is no good. Mine is still strong, even if some chips have been struck away.

There are five objectives in these Affirmations:

- to persuade some who have chucked overboard their earlier religious beliefs, to pause, take another look, and reconsider;
- to encourage those who have stayed inside faith in God despite struggles within and without;
- to hope that the dogmatically minded may find an ounce of charity that will make room in the family of faith for those of us who do not see things exactly as

they do;

- to entice some who have never ventured into Christian faith to take that leap of faith; and
- to have a partnership with the reader . . . but who wants a partner who agrees with everything (in which case one of them isn't thinking)?

After all, thinking about God and Christian faith is autobiography—one person's effort to find validity for his or her place in it.

The *compressing* of belief has nothing to do with any *diminishing* of faith. There is a difference between belief and faith. Sometimes one may question a belief, or discard it altogether. But one goes on with faith.

Perhaps a lessening of belief is because in younger years too many things were taken for granted. Too often I heard, "That's the way it is!" and uncritically accepted that. That same dogmatism is too much with us today. Then I saw (and see) other Christians who did not believe that way, but who were devout in their faith and practice. That meant some beliefs had to be examined. As a result, some beliefs were diminished and some were eliminated.

The premise of "living in tension," with which I have approached life personally and professionally, began in college. The thread of that tension will be found in this uneven tapestry called "affirmations." College courses in philosophy taught various philosophies of life. Two of those were Idealism and Pragmatism. I began looking at myself as an "idealistic pragmatist" or as a "pragmatic idealist." Thus the "tensions" between the ideal and the actual, the ought and the is, things as they should be and things as they are. The task is to bring the two closer together step by achievable step, knowing that we shall never succeed. . . . But we must try.

These chapters are presented under the umbrella "Affirmations of a Skeptical Believer." The approach is positive. This is not a book of theology, although there are theological undertones and overtones.

This is not "an after-retirement safety net." I have often been aloft, not knowing whether there was a net or not. When caught between the Scylla of a denomination's doctrinal orthodoxy and the Charybdis of personal integrity, what does one do? I could have adopted the fence-sitting neutrality of a "mugwump," facetiously described as one who sits with his mug on one side and his wump on the other, with the result that one's tail gets caught in a crack and pinched on both sides. It is better to be one or the other.

Shakespeare has some good advice in *Hamlet,* via Polonius to Laertes: "To thine own self be true." Even this has limitations: to which self and for what reasons? To me, it is to be true to one's self in the light of belief in and commitment of life to God. In my case, the best possible understanding of God in the Christian ministry.

Success is not in having everyone's approval, though I have my share of desiring approval. Success is rather in the pursuit of one's calling to the best of one's ability, and realizing whatever potential so that life is harmonious. Christianity should not be a pallid, censorious, joyless way of life, but a zestful, venturesome realization of its finest possibilities. And people can find the way to the Christian life by diverse routes, with Jesus Christ as the common denominator.

Nothing is said in these pages that was not said to churches where I was pastor. Those people listened patiently. They shared their own affirmations and uncertainities. They did not always agree with me. Some thought me too liberal, others too conservative. But they let me be myself, and their faith was strengthened and enabled them to be themselves. So I express appreciation to those churches: First Baptist in Ruston, Louisiana; St. Charles Avenue Baptist in New Orleans; and University Bapitst in Hattiesburg,

Mississippi.

This book is written with five friends in mind. They are representative of the human spectrum of belief and skepticism. I was drawn to them by strange circumstances. I am the only one who knows them all. Each has heard of the others from me. They share the classification of "kindred spirits." We have talked and corresponded about the issues in these pages. Four have read the manuscript. Naturally, they are not in full agreement. None would object to being identified, but to preserve their privacy, only their first names shall be used, with the length of friendship in parentheses.

Sam (47) is a Baptist with a doctoral degree in education. He can be acerbic and irascible, while at the same time he is sensitive and compassionate, at his best with questioning collegians. His theology is basically moderate. He thinks, probes, and prods in a mental honesty that is understanding of other positions.

Bruce (42) is a reverently agnostic physician who is a true humanitarian. He is half Jewish, with a discarded Presbyterian upbringing. At age 68 he finally joined a Methodist church. Ever the pragmatist, he said, "I wouldn't want to live in a place where there were no churches. To be consistent, I should join a church, if I could find one that would take me as I am. If I belong to a church, I ought to support it, and I do."

John (29) is a Christian educator, the founder of an outstanding private elementary-secondary school. He has a literal belief about the Bible and all the fundamentalist doctrines. In spirit, he is not a Fundamentalist who would impose his beliefs on anyone else. However a person identifies with the Christian faith is acceptable with John.

Dick (21) is a premier makeup artist who has won top awards in every arena of the entertainment industry. He calls himself an atheist, although he has a New York Episcopal background. He is a humanist who would do right because it is right, and be good for goodness' sake. And he does. Both he and Bruce have a strong sense of the mystical.

Frank (15) has a doctoral degree in English Literature. He was a university professor. Now he is an advertising executive and aspiring playwright-novelist, living in New York City. If one can be a skeptical, yet devout Roman Catholic, Frank is.

A good word to describe these friends is "acceptance." They accept themselves as they are, me as I am, and others as they are. We all have trouble with dogmatists of any kind. There is a place for each of them in the Christian faith. Each of their lives gives evidence of concern for the world and its people, and they try to make life better. They are men of personal integrity. I trust them implicity. We seldom see each other, once or twice a year at most; Dick only eight times in two decades. Yet, with each one there is an uncanny closeness that I cannot describe. Anyone who has such a friend will understand.

A sixth person needs to be added: Gladys Salassi Lee, my wife of sixteeen years and friend whom I both love and like. She is a student and teacher of French language and literature who has come through Hugo, Voltaire, Ionesco, Camus, Sartre, et al., with her faith confidently intact.

A special word of thanks goes to Mrs. George (Valerie) Pierce who typed the first draft of this manuscript, and to Mrs. Ruth Deuchert who typed the final copy.

You are invited to come along and merge with your own affirmations.

—*G. Avery Lee*, Pastor Emeritus
St. Charles Avenue Baptist Church
New Orleans
1991

✝ An Agnostic Can Be a Christian

Some years ago I preached a sermon entitled "An Agnostic Can Be a Christian." A prominent New Orleans lawyer from another church, who only saw the subject in a newspaper and did not hear the sermon, took me to task, saying that the terms *agnostic* and *Christian* are mutually exclusive. He wrote,

> An agnostic is not—cannot be—a Christian at the same time. One is either an agnostic or a Christian, but he most assuredly is not both simultaneously.

I disagreed with him then, and I do now.

Yes, I believe an agnostic can be a Christian. I know some. There is a trace of the agnostic or skeptic in each of us, more in some than in others. Skepticism is not an assault on Christian faith; it is rather a form of affirmation. There are some skeptical believers. I am one of them.

Erasmus, who—it has been said—laid the egg that Martin Luther hatched, may have been the first Christian agnostic, for he was skeptical of many of Rome's "articles of faith." Erasmus was certainly the first Christian humanist, terms which many today think are mutually exclusive, but are not.

The first time I remember ever hearing the term "Christian agnostic" was in a class at the Yale Divinity School more than forty-five years ago when Professor Millar Burrows described himself as being "a reverent Christian agnostic." Professor Burrows was a devout Christian and a renowned Old Testament scholar. In 1966 Leslie Weatherhead published a book entitled *The Christian Agnostic*.[1] That title describes many people I know, admire, and believe in. My alter ego is such a person.

By agnostic I do not mean the atheist who says there is no God. I have met very few persons who are out-and-out atheists. I suspect most of them could be pinned down to admitting that *no* God is not exactly what they mean. We have too often made the mistake of equating the atheist and the agnostic. Perhaps one reason for this is the standard dictionary definition of the agnostic as "one who holds that nothing is known or likely to be known of the existence of God," or "one who holds that the ultimate cause and the essential nature of things are unknown and unknowable . . . an intellectual doctrine or attitude affirming the uncertainty of all claims of ultimate knowledge."

In using the term "Christian Agnostic" or "Agnostic Christian," I am referring to a person who is immensely attracted to Jesus, who seeks to show his spirit, who tries to meet the challenges and problems of life in that spirit, and feels that although he is sure of many Christian truths, he cannot honestly and conscientiously "sign on the dotted

---

[1]Leslie D. Weatherhead, *The Christian Agnostic* (New York and Nashville: Abingdon Press, 1966).

line" for church membership because he cannot believe all of the theological ideas of Christian faith. Somehow— wrongly I think—he feels that the church excludes him because he cannot believe. His intellectual integrity causes him to say about many things, "It may be so, but I do not know for sure."

Many of these people feel that church services are dull and irrelevant. Many have been put off by the frailties of church members. Many no longer can believe what the church says it believes and feel their intellectual integrity would be impugned by joining the church. On the other hand, there are perhaps just as many who, while being honest with themselves about such things, are not equally honest with themselves in some matters of personal conduct and use a form of honest doubt to cover up some forms of substandard behavior.

I believe Christianity is a way of life more than it is a system of intellectual assent. This does not mean that one can believe just anything and be a Christian. There are some basic areas of belief that are a part of Christian faith. But I do feel that Jesus himself would admit and welcome anyone who sincerely desired to follow him, whether he understood all about him or not. Jesus did this, in fact, more than once. He even took Peter on lesser terms than he desired.

We can see much of this in other Christians. From the doctrinaire Roman Catholic to the quiet Quaker, from the high-church Episcopalian to the fervent Pentecostalist, and all varieties in between, it is clear that all beliefs about Christian faith and all Christian experiences are not the same. These people are Christian. Let no one deny that. They have found something in Jesus Christ that is meaningful and significant to them. Some of what one believes, another would doubt and another discard altogether. The approach that one takes, another would never consider. In this we see the broad inclusiveness of Christian faith.

There are some dissimilarities, of course, but there are even more similarities. With some we could clasp hands in united fellowship, with others we would hold back in reservation, and with some we would find it difficult to walk. But walk we do, and walk we must . . . for they are not our enemies. As John Wesley put it,

> Whoever follows Christ is my brother.

Or as the hymn "In Christ There Is No East or West" says,

> Who serves my Father . . . is surely kin to me.

And even better, what Jesus said,

> Whoever is not against us is for us.   —Mark 9:40 NRSV

We must not sneer at their creeds, nor disdain the ancient creeds that some used to believe, and some still do. Harry Emerson Fosdick said he had "never subscribed to . . . nor repeated" the Apostles Creed or any other.[2] He

---

[2]Fosdick, in *The Modern Use of the Bible*, Lyman Beecher Lectures 1923-1924 (New York: Macmillan Co., 1924), wrote that "it is a pity that even in churches which are not bound to these eccelsiastical creeds of the patristic age [Apostles',Nicene, and Athanasian Creeds], we cannot have a better understanding of what they really meant to say. Personally brought up in an ecclesiastical tradition which has not used these venerable expressions. *I have never subscribed to them nor repeated them*. But, standing thus outside the tradition to which these creeds belong, when I hear some fresh and flippant modern mind condescending to them, treating the fathers who wrote them as quibblers and fools, *I am strongly tempted to bear a hand in their defense*." (262, emphasis added)

could not and would not say that he believed all that it said, therefore, he could not repeat it. Nor do I believe everything the creeds say. But I have repeated them, with reservations, as ancient affirmations of faith.

We must remember those ancient creeds were written to rebut then-current charges, not to impose a formula of belief for all future generations. Just as David could not fight Goliath in Saul's armor, so we must outfit ourselves in the armor that fits us as we do battle with today's Goliaths.

On the other hand, some things need to go, for they are "Saul's armor." We must not set up unnecessary barriers nor erect walls of hindrance to those who are honestly seeking the way of Jesus Christ . . . honestly seeking, that is, with the emphasis on both words. We have added a lot of unneeded trimmings to the simple New Testament statement "Jesus Christ is Lord."

Unless we can break out of the prisons of old-fashioned expressions and creeds, we shall never be free to find far more glorious truths of the Christian faith. Of all people, we of the "Free Church" tradition, who have never been a creedal people, ought to believe and practice this. Yet there are some who insist on trying to make everyone conform to a mold—*their mold.*

Every effort to express Christian faith will be full of half-truths and mistakes, and much will be left unsaid because we just do not know. There will be large areas of "reverent agnosticism" where we must say, "I just don't know." Or, better, "Lord, I believe, help my unbelief." Listen to Robert Browning:

> God's gift was that man should conceive of truth
> And yearn to gain it, catching at mistake,
> As midway help till he reach fact indeed.
>
> —from "A Death in the Desert"

Jerald Savory, pastor of the Judson Baptist Church in

Kalamazoo, Michigan, related an experience he once had:

> The other day I was standing near the elevator in a local hospital when my eye was captured by a sign partly visible around the corner from where I stood. It read, AGNOSTIC SERVICES. Curious about whether the hospital had taken on a counseling program for the uncommitted, I walked around the corner and read the sign again. Now I could see all of it, it read DIAGNOSTIC SERVICES. It was a sign indicating the room where examinations are made in the hope of determining the nature and circumstances of certain diseased conditions. It is a place for diagnosis, an essential medical procedure prior to the physician's recommendation for treatment.[3]

Each of us knows that this aspect of medicine, necessary as it is, produces a lot of tension because the cure of the patient depends upon the accuracy of the diagnosis. A hasty or faulty diagnosis that fails to probe every possibility may mean the difference between health and illness—even life or death—for the patient. Also, even the most thorough examination does not guarantee that full cure can be effected. Sometimes the doctor must take a calculated risk, not having all the evidence he would like to have, yet knowing he has to do something. Diagnosis is a heavy responsibility on the doctor who does not give it priority, not for fear of a malpractice suit, but because he wants to bring healing, if he can.

Both signs in that hospital have significance. The word "agnostic" and the word "diagnostic" refer to knowledge *before* and *after* as well as *during* the searching probe for truth. A person involved in diagnosis is one in search of truth about a patient's condition in the hope that an avenue

---

[3]*The Pulpit* (April 1967): 23.

of healing may be found. By the same token, an agnostic is one who is in search of the truth that gives meaning to life.

Perhaps the one major difference is that sooner or later the physician must do the best he can with the alternatives he sees, even if there is risk involved. On the other hand, the agnostic may not see the need to make a decision. He remains committed to one thing only: the affirmation that he is not committed to any one thing.

The Christian church is in existence because its members have made a kind of diagnosis about the meaning of life which centers in the belief that life's meaning has been given and is best seen in Jesus of Nazareth. It often appears that, having come to this conclusion, churches have sometimes closed their diagnostic doors to any further probing, thus looking upon the honest skeptic as a threat to the life of the church.

On the other hand, many a skeptical agnostic has closed his diagnostic door in that he refuses to take the step of calculated risk on what he alreay knows. He fails to recognize that the church, and Christians, have made a lot of advances since he last took a look or a step, and he is not willing to look at the new evidence and take that further step.

I said earlier that I did not want to water down any of the truths of Chrstian faith, that there are some basics. This book is a statement of some of those basics. I do not feel bound by old dogmas, nor do I want to be shackled by this summary statement. There is so much to learn, to know, to experience, and to practice about the Christian faith and life. It is a never-ending process. Beware of anyone who says he or she has *arrived.*

I would say to any who might classify themselves with the agnostics, the Christian agnostics,

Don't exclude yourself from the fellowship of Jesus' followers because of some mental reservations. We all have some of those.

In the meantime, be as the physician who takes the calculated risk. Join with those who are trying to spread this spirit of Christ.

A prayer

*Almighty God,
forgive me my agnosticism,
for I shall try to keep it gentle,
not cynical, not a bad influence.*

*If Thou are truly in the heavens,
accept my gratitude
for all Thy gifts
and I shall try
to fight the good fight.
Amen.*

—JOHN GUNTHER, JR.

✝ God Is

The man sitting across from me was in his sixties, ten years my junior. He was a tenured university professor who had driven one hundred miles for the conversation. After a hour of talk about matters of long-time acquaintance, his academic career, and his thoughts of a professional change, he finally got to the point of the visit. In a soft voice, and with a wistful look, he said, "Avery, tell me honestly what you believe about God."

I began with a story.

The most versatile computer the world had ever seen was placed on display. This computer had been fed the distilled knowledge of the centuries. The greatest minds of the world—theologians, philosophers, scientists, poets, artists, journalists—all the great thinkers had gathered to marvel at this phenomenon. They all agreed that the most vital question they had all wondered about would be posed to the computer. So they asked, "Is there a God?" After some whirling noises, the computer answered, "There is now!"

The issue is not the existence of God, but the *significance* of God. God is not a problem to be solved by a computer. God is a mystery to be experienced. Always has been, always will be.

The Bible neither offers an explanation for the origin of God, nor does it present arguments for the existence of the reality of God. It *assumes* that *God is*. The Bible is a record of people who, for the most part, believe in God and of the ways God works in their life and in their world. The Bible also records their struggles to continue to believe.

Either a person believes in God, or does not. People believe in God for a variety of reasons. Some believe because belief provides a logical explanation for the universe, earth, and life on earth; others, because belief satisfies an inner need for security. Still others believe because a foundation for moral-ethical behavior thus is furnished.

Those who do not believe have as many reasons. They say such belief is superstitious nonsense, illogical and irrelevant, that believers are merely projecting their own ideals and values and calling them God. One often wonders if the unbelievers still have a wistful residue of faith. Something is in life that is beyond the human mind and will. Faith in God is not so much believing "the evidence of things not seen," as it is believing in *the things for which there is no proof.*

I believe in God. Always have. Well, for more than six decades I have. Prior to that I had no knowledge of God, one way or the other. At age twelve I was introduced to God on a limited basis. I've been on the journey of faith ever since. This God in whom I believe may not be the same for you. That's because God is God.

The God in whom I believe now is not the same as at the beginning. There have been many changes *in me* in the interim. I am a strict monotheist: "Hear, O Israel: the Lord our God is *one* Lord." My belief in God has been a process of adaptive assimilation. That means some lesser gods, or limited concepts of God, have been shed.

As wider skies broke on his view.
God greatened in his growing mind;
Each year he dreamed his God anew,
And left his older god behind.
—Sam Walter Foss, "A Philosopher"

I've had some doubts along the way. There are some beliefs about God I cannot accept. These have been discarded as unessential. But belief in a Supreme Being whom we call God? Yes! More firmly now than ever.

But what do I really believe and feel about God? After more than a half century of study and preaching, I'm not sure. There is a firm belief that *God is*. The universe, the world, and the people in it make little sense without God. It is easy to intellectualize God; internalizing God is another matter. This God in whom I believe is not the God of my youth—a wrathful diety who desires vengeance—nor some celestial Santa Claus who gives us good things if we are good, not even some heavenly bookkeeper who keeps score on our good and bad deeds. I didn't quite believe that then, but that is what I heard, and still hear from many sources.

What is God to me? What do I actually feel? That God is love? Yes, but that is abstract. That God cares for me? Yes, but not to the extent of changing the universe to placate my whims or satisfy my desires. That God has the whole world in his hands? Yes, but some things that happen in this world do not square with loving and caring. This means that God has "limited" himself. There are some things not even God can do. Even so, God *must* have something to do with our existence, our life; something, "a power, not ourselves, that makes for righteousness," that reinforces and enables us to rise above circumstances and become truly human . . . *in the best sense.*

Sometimes I fantasize about what I would say if ever there came a chance to speak with God. Among other things, I would ask, "God, is everything they say about you on earth true?" And I imagine God answering with a soft smile, a twinkle in his eyes, and a gentle voice, "No, son, but they mean well."

I have studied some philosophy and theology, although I am neither a philosopher nor a theologian. Philosophers and theologians seek answers to the *whys* of earth and life. The philosophical arguments for the existence of God—that God is—may make sense, but they are not proof.

Anyone who tries to answer some of life's *whys* is a philosopher. Theological arguments of *what* God is are as numerous as the philosophers' *whys*. But, again, not proof. Theology is nothing more than the autobiography of one person wrestling with the meaning of God in his or her life. Scientists search for the *how* of that "First Cause," but they can scarcely improve on the Genesis account. The ultimately conclusive argument for the existence of God is empirical. It is in an experience, rational or mystic, that the reality of God is found.

I don't know exactly what I believed about God at the beginning. Probably nothing more than the average adolescent who is told that there is a God, and perhaps a vague kind of inner acknowledgement. The God with whom I began as a lad remained limitedly the same throughout high school. That God was relatively simple, and my concepts were simplistic. College brought some quiet examinations, but not much change. Then I experienced a cultural and religious shock in going from Oklahoma–West Texas to Connecticut and the Yale University Divinity School. That began a lot of change, for I was but shortly out of a Pentecostal background. It was not a trauma of rebellion, but more of a realization that many things were missing. My God was too small.

It is easy to drift along in a routine religious life without any serious thought until the time when we meet up with something that doesn't fit, or presents an obstacle. Then we must expand our thinking with some new insights. Scientific change comes that way. So should our thinking and understanding of God.

In music there is the term *dissonance*—a disagreement in sound, an inharmonious sound, or a harsh discord. That dissonance hangs in the air until it is resolved to a harmonious sound. Some modern music, which reflects the moods of the times, ends in dissonance (Anton von Webern, for example). But we listen and learn. Music without its dissonances would often be bland. Our understanding of God is that way. We cannot explain all the mysteries and disharmonies, but on occasion there does come a harmonious resolution.

To achieve a more worthy conception of God has always been the challenge of religion. Every generation is faced with the problem of more adequate concepts of God. The glory of the Judeo-Christian tradition lies in having done that in all generations. God has never been static for them. We must never allow any idea of God to become fixed.

Each generation considers its views to be more enlightened than the previous one(s). We may not improve on the understandings of God that past generations had, but we do begin with that earlier understanding, and then proceed to our own. Our notions of God mesh with our moment in history, in all kinds of complicated ways. When we are the one trying to pin the tail on the donkey in the parlor game, we don't know how close we've come until we take off the blindfold. We are still wearing blindfolds when it comes to knowing God. But we must try to know for ourselves, even if we cannot know all there is to know about

God.

The Bible itself is a development of expanding beliefs, concepts, and understanding of God. God remains the same, but different facets and attributes are forthcoming because of man's changing perceptions.

What we understand about God today is a far cry from those days when Yahweh (Jehovah), the God of the Hebrews, was associated with a mountain called Sinai. Across the years the Hebrews enlarged this concept of God. Although Palestine is only about the size of Louisiana, to them it seemed a big place. As they had worshipped God on Mount Sinai, now they worshipped God on every hill in Canaan. In fact, at that time all gods were geographically limited. That is what David alluded to when, being driven out by King Saul to the Philistine cities, he cried,

> "They have driven me out this day that I should have no share in the heritage of the Lord [Yahweh], saying, 'Go, serve other gods.' " —1 Samuel 26:19

We often get sentimental over the memorable words that Ruth spoke to Naomi. In the sentiment we forget just how significant those words really were. Ruth, living in Moab, had worshipped Moab's god, Chemosh. But in Bethlehem, Yahweh was God. So she said to her mother-in-law Naomi,

> "Entreat me not to leave thee, or to return [turn away] from following after thee; for whither thou goest, I will go; and where thou lodgest, I will lodge; thy people shall be my people, and thy God, my God." —Ruth 1:16

Change countries . . . change gods. As late as the Babylonian Exile, some four centuries after David, the idea of a geographic god was still present: "How shall we sing the Lord's song in a strange land?" (Psalm 137:4)

As lines of travel, trade, and communication developed, people could not keep their gods geographically located. In earlier days, Moses had grappled with a truth which led him to believe there was but one God in all the universe.

> (This is a concept that may have come from the Egyptians. Before the Exodus, Pharoah Ikhnaton [or Akhenaton] tried to establish a kind of monotheism. It was short-lived, but must have had some believers. Perhaps Moses was one. He certainly had access to the idea.)

The Hebrew people professed belief in One God, but it took them a long time to see that this one God was not exclusively theirs, but was the God of all the people in the world.

There were other things they needed to know about God. They felt that the earth was flat. Heaven was above and Sheol (later, Hell) was below the earth. What did God have to do with that? They would not allow God to stay that small, and the Psalmist declared,

> If I ascend up into heaven, thou art there; if I make my bed in sheol, behold, thou art there. If I take the wings of the morning, and dwell in the uttermost parts of the sea; even there shall thy hand lead me, and thy right hand shall hold me.   —Psalm 139:8-10

That 139th Psalm represents a profound enlargement of the idea of God. He was God, not simply of all the earth, but of the heavens above, of the abode of the dead—indeed, God of all the universe. One of the most exquisite poems in the English language, Francis Thompson's "The Hound of Heaven," is based on this psalm.[1]

---

[1]As found in, e.g., *Modern British Poetry*, 4th rev. ed., ed. Louis Untermeyer (New York: Harcourt Brace and Co., 1936) 149.

But that universe would not remain so cozy, with the earth as the center. Copernicus, Galileo, and Kepler came along. The universe became incredibly vast, and distances were unbelievable. Multitudes thought and were afraid that they would have to give up on God. That's why they fought this new idea so hard. But man did not give up God. Man did what he has always done: he enlarged and deepened his concept of God.

It is unfortunate that so often in history anything new—that is, change—has been opposed by men who earnestly believe in God, but whose concept of God is narrow. It is even so today. But God will not be confined. Today's "Creationists" do God no service when they try to limit him to their own concepts. In reality, they diminish the broadness of God.

Today the situation of an enlarged universe faces us again. The birth of the atomic/space age has revealed a universe that is law-abiding beyond our ability to think, a world both infinite and infinitesimal. Now we are exploring what is called outer space. As usual, there are those who say that our earthbound ideas of God are so outmoded that God must be abandoned.

One of Russia's early cosmonauts said he did not see either heaven or God, therefore, there must not be such a place or such a person. In the 1961 Moscow "Christmas Broadcast" it was said that "The achievements of a non-existent God are colorless before the achievements of Soviet man."

This sort of thing has happened since Eden and Sinai, Copernicus and Galileo. Some may look up and say, "There is no God." But always there have been those who stand in reverence before a vaster universe, saying, "The Lord sits above the circle of the earth."

Contrast the Russian cosmonaut's statement with that of American astronaut James A. McDivitt, who orbited the earth sixty-two times aboard Gemini 4:

> I did not see God looking into my space cabin window,
> as I do not see God looking into my car's windshield. But
> I could recognize His work in the stars as well as when
> I'm walking among flowers in a garden.

One either believes in God or does not. Belief is neither proved by an astronaut, nor disproved by a cosmonaut.

There is another area where the idea of God had to deepen and mature. It is closely allied with the geographic-god idea. The early Hebrews jealously guarded their belief that Yahweh, while being the God of the universe, was exclusively theirs. The Moabites, Philistines, and Egyptians were left out. It was hard for them to come to see that this God of the universe was the God of all people as well. The Book of Jonah shows that the stubborn resistance to offering salvation to other than the Jews was a reality. But a reluctant Jonah finally did come to see the universality of God, even though he didn't want to. Jonah pouted because he did not want to share his God with Ninevah, nor did he really want Ninevah to repent.

Even in the New Testament there were those who could not accept the message that God's "good news" was for all—Jew, Greek, barbarian, free and slave, male and female. It took a dedicated Jew, Saul of Tarsus, who was willing to face a hostile world and say,

> I am not ashamed of the gospel of Christ; for it is the
> power of God unto salvation to *everyone* that believeth.
> —Romans 1:16

So Paul, and others, despite opposition, reached out to grasp the spiritual idea of God, and they expressed it in such words as

> . . . he is not far from every one of us; for in him we live
> and move, and have our being. . . .   —Acts 17:27-28

The story of the development of the idea of God is an ever-continuing one. We have not seen the end of it, even if we Christians do claim the ultimate revelation of God in Jesus Christ. God has not yet spoken His final words. No one of us can say that we have put into practice what little we do know of God. No one person, no group of persons, no one generation can ever know all there is to know of God. We must always meet each new situation in each new day with an enlarging and deepening of our understanding of God, and demonstrate more fully what we already know.

To do this, we must not be upset by "growing pains" of any kind, especially those pains of growing that involve the religious life. There are some in the religious life, or Christian faith, who are satisfied with what they have and neither want nor seem to need anything more. For them, that may be all right. But for me there is a kind of divine dissatisfaction that wants and needs more. Growth and development are normal parts of *every* phase of life, personal or social, for a person, a people, or a nation. An athletic cliché says "No pain, no gain." I believe that holds true for one's religious life.

The discomfort of growth is irritating and sometimes expensive. But it is worthwhile. Mankind is, on the whole, lazy, especially in religious matters. We would prefer not to think. We may even want to stop progressing. The hardest of all work is thinking, especially when thinking means we may have to remove some old concepts and get on with some new, enlarged ones. It may be comfortable if we could say about God that we have the final thought about Him, that we shall never have to think about Him again. And there are those who tell us that.

Who wants it that way? Some do. I do not. Were we to stop with the geographical god,

with the god of the old astronomy,
    with the god that excludes some,
        with a god whom our finite minds make finite,
we would have a limited God.

Those who study bees, estimate that a pound of honey costs 40,000 flying miles on the part of the bees. A family might eat a pound of honey during one breakfast of waffles as a matter of course. But at what cost to the bees! Just so, every advancing idea of God has cost its own 40,000 miles.

The process of growth is confusing and costly. Socrates was called an atheist because he denied the contemporary idea of a pantheon of deities on Mount Olympus. They made him drink hemlock as an atheist. But he was not an atheist. He did not know God as we know Him, but he did advance, and we now accept many of his ideas. The early Christians were called atheists because they denied the then-current idea of many gods. They were flung to the lions because they held firm to the One True God.

All of this was a part of the growing pains of the past. We need not be afraid of similar pains today. Our generation faces new problems, or at least some old problems in new dress. Russia, which proclaims that the idea of God is made obsolete by man's modern achievements, would be an example. Another example is the thinking that religion is to meet our own needs of security and success, the mindset that has made Christianity a "cultural religion."

Some modern existentialists, such as Sartre and Heidegger or Altizer and Hamilton, who took their cue from Nietzsche, have said, "God is dead." For some, God is not dead, but He may be in eclipse. As the late Jewish philosopher, Martin Buber, put it, "The eclipse of the light of God is no extinction; even tomorrow that which has stepped in may give way."[2]

God is not dead. Our generation will not give up God. Nor will God be limited or made to fit our narrow notions.

We should recognize that to our limited and finite minds the fullness of God is incomprehensible. No one can adequately grasp all there is of God.

This infiniteness of God requires our finite minds to use symbols as a means of expression. There are those who criticize us for use of the symbolic. What else can we do? Mathematics, music, chemistry, physics—all use symbols to express ideas that are beyond words. We can't even express all our human emotions without the use of symbols:

a handshake;

a kiss between lovers, family, or friends;

the flag of one's country.

When we think of this great God, we take some element of our own experience and use it to help us understand. We may say that God is our Rock, our Fortress, our Sure Foundation. And let us not be criticized for this.

One of the early explorers of America was named Giovanni da Verrazano. He looked out across Chesapeake Bay and thought it was the Pacific Ocean. Dare we laugh at him? Of course not. In many details he was right. There *is* a Pacific Ocean. He had the right direction. The Pacific Ocean was thousands of miles farther on, but he was headed right. It is far truer to think of the Pacific Ocean in terms of Chesapeake Bay than it is to deny the Pacific Ocean altogether.

Here is a man bowing before some image. I cannot do that. But see what he may be doing—thinking of the Pacific Ocean in terms of Chesapeake Bay. Inadequate as that is, it is better than denying the Pacific's reality. We who do be-

---

[2]Martin Buber, *The Eclipse of God: Studies in the Relation between Religion and Philosophy*, trans. Maurice S. Friedman (New York: Harper & Bros., 1952) 129.

lieve in God should try to show God to him, instead of letting him remain at Chesapeake with his image.

Let us recognize that some of our thoughts about God are inadequate, sometimes even childish. Many among us are thus tempted to give up God altogether. But that is a wrong approach. It is better to think of God in inadequate symbols than not to think of Him at all. *God is.* Our ideas of Him are partial.

People have said to me, "I am an atheist," sometimes facetiously adding, "thank God." Usually what such a person is denying is not God, but some outmoded idea of God that some of us already have discarded. We have a responsibility to be patient and assist such a person to get rid of his or her little gods and make room for Him of whom the Bible tells us and whom our experience confirms.

My entire ministry has been with a college-related church. Many times students, fresh from some early science, philosophy, or sociology course, have come to my office and—perhaps thinking to shock me—have said, "Dr. Lee, I do not believe in God."

Nothing really shocks me—startles perhaps, but not shocks. My stock reply has been, "Tell me about this god in whom you do not believe."

Then there is some convoluted logic about the six days of Creation and geology, or Virgin Birth and parthenogenesis, or some such. After they have spoken, my usual reply is, "I don't believe in that kind of a god, either."

Such statements are not limited to college students. A brilliant surgeon asked me to lunch. During lunch he said, "Avery, I no longer believe in God. I want you to remove my name from the church roll."

I asked him to tell me why he did not believe in God. After he had finished, I said, "Dr. _____, you are talking about things you should have dealt with as a sophomore in college."

God is great, very great . . . too great for our little minds to grasp. But there is the fact that God has a "near end" where He literally touches us. Those of us who grew up on the great plains of the Southwest would not know such a term as "near end." It belongs to those who live by the sea. A small island is off the coast. The water around that little island is not the whole sea. The sea is much larger than that. But one living on the island can know the sea for, where it touches that island, the sea has a "near end."

So has God. So great, so vast, so infinite. But God has a "near end" that touches us. How?

Those of Judaism feel the touch of God in the Law, in the prophets, in their historic heritage, in their scriptures, and in their destiny. We Christians share that with them. But for us there is something more. We Christians believe that in Jesus of Nazareth, God touched our island. That is, "the Word became flesh and dwelt among us, full of grace and truth" (John 1:14).

It is true we cannot understand all of what we teach in the doctrine we call the Incarnation. But we can grasp something of the Hebrew word "Immanuel"—*God with us*.

Jesus came into the world that we might have some touch of God. I do not believe that all of God was in Jesus of Nazareth. But I do believe that in Jesus Christ God washes our little island. There God reaches. There we can touch the "near end" of God.[3]

---

[3]The "near end" illustration is from Harry Emerson Fosdick, in his sermon "The Greatness of God," as reprinted in *Riverside Sermons*, 255-64 (New York: Harper & Bros., 1958) 262-63. Fosdick concluded that "Of course this is what the 'divinity' of Jesus means. . . . No intelligent theology ever meant by the 'divinity' of Jesus what some people think is implied in it, but this it does mean, that in

Through the centuries there has been theological conflict over the "doctrine of God." Classic orthodoxy, along with neoorthodoxy and fundamentalism, emphasizes the *transcendence* of God—an all-powerful, remote force, rather arbitrarily doing as he pleases, for such a God is above the laws of nature and science. Classic liberalism and its newer forms stress the *immanence* of God—that is, a more personal, present presence that is in us all at all times and in everything.

There are traces of strength in both of these positions, just as there are limitations. There is a place for both a transcendent and an immanent God, a God who is neither tyrant nor softhearted, a God of ordered discipline and of compassionate love. There need not be an either/or, but rather a both/and. The formula of thesis-antithesis-synthesis finds a middle ground that recognizes the "divine spark" that is in every human personality. Orthodoxy can help preserve the values of the past, while liberalism keeps us from being rooted in the past by adapting to new circumstances.

I like the concept of a personal God that is seen in Tevye's talks with God in *Fiddler on the Roof.* I want God to be that way, and believe that He is. It is true that we often make God too austere and remote, some kind of a majestic holiness. On the other hand, we can just as easily go to the other extreme with casual references to "The Man Upstairs." Such a cursory attitude looks upon God as a kind of divine Santa Claus who keeps us in line, or a Celestial Vending Machine into which we put a quarter's worth of expectancy, push a button, and look for the package to fall out. If it doesn't, we kick the machine (God) and demand our money (faith) back.

the spiritual life and character of Christ we touch the near end of God. There God reaches us. There he washes our island." (263)

Christian history is studded with sincere, reverent mystics who seemingly had an unusual closeness to God— St. Augustine, Meister Eckehart, Count Zinzendorf, Brother Lawrence, and Frank Laubach, to name a few. I would not deny the validity of their experiences. Nor do I begrudge them. However, there is a tendency toward elitism in many of today's mystics.

Many people seem to believe that God speaks to them . . . directly. I do think God can speak to us, though not verbally. But what if God says something to me that is quite different from what He said to you? One of us might need a new hearing aid. It certainly causes complications when we try to defend what we say we have heard. I've always been suspicious of anyone who says, "God said to me. . . . "

A man I know was a member of the board of trustees of a Baptist college. The college needed a new president, so a search committee was appointed. The committee searched. The trustees met to hear the report of their search. The chairman said, "We have prayed long and hard, and God has said to us, 'This is the man for you.' "

Whereupon another trustee arose and spoke, "I too have prayed long and hard, and God said to me, 'This is *not* the man for you.' "

And there was much discussion about what God had said to whom. When we assume a too-close relationship to God, we are susceptible to equating ourselves with God.

Does having a mystical experience make one a better Christian? Does not having it make one a lesser Christian? Do those who do not have the experience just not believe strongly enough, or not have enough faith? No. I can't accept or believe that. People are different. The identical experience is not required of everyone.

Many Christians are made to feel guilty, made to feel as if they are missing out on someting if they don't have such an experience. And there is a tendency among those who do to say they feel sorry for those of us who do not. It seems to me it would be more of a virtue if such feelings were concealed.

I have never had such an experience. Maybe I wouldn't recognize it if I did. There have been times in retrospect when experiences had a connection that caused things to fit together and perhaps the only explanation is that God—or someone—had a hand in it. Sometimes I've felt as if I'd like to be a mystic, but my skeptical, pragmatic nature doesn't allow for that. But I've never felt myself any less Christian because of how I am—for other reasons, perhaps, but not that. If the mystical experience is the gift of God, then some of us just have not received it. I don't mind not having the mystical experience, but I don't want to be considered a second-class Christian because of that.

Let's take this idea a step further. There are people who derive comfort from thinking of God as a friendly neighbor, one of the "good ol' boys." We do need to think of God as our friend: he is certainly not our enemy. It's natural to think of God in human terms, what the theologians call "anthropomorphizing" God. We tend to think in terms of what we can visualize. Some are able to think in the abstract, but most of us cannot. Most of us cannot think in terms of "Spirit." We need something more concrete.

I do believe in a feeling of the "nearness" of God. But there is a dangerous temptation here for us to try and "cash in" on the relationship by trying to possess God and use Him to our advantage. If we had such a relationship as that, God would not be God anymore. He would become an object, an acquaintance with clout. And sooner or later we would be looking for someone with more clout, especially if we ever felt let down or didn't get what we wanted.

God cannot be and is not to be manipulated. To appeal to God to validate our thinking, purposes, or desires is a kind of idolatry. It is an irresponsible effort to use God to serve our ends. This is not only not right, but it shows little respect for God. Do you remember the bumper sticker that said "God is my copilot"? . . . That reduces God to being an assistant with second-place status.

In both Romans and Corinthians, Paul says that a proper understanding of our responsibilities within the Christian community of believers will save us from pride in whatever of God's gifts we may possess; likewise it will save us from shame for any gift we may lack (Rom. 12:3-8; 1 Cor. 12:1-31).

God's gifts are not for our private enjoyment, although we may enjoy them. Using a gift in any way that may disrupt the fellowship or cause another to feel left out is not right. There is a variety of gifts and God is the giver of them all. Therefore, there should be no unseemly pride or boasting among those who seem to be more richly endowed than others; nor should there be any feeling of inferiority on the part of those who consider themselves to be less endowed.

What this boils down to gets to where I make a decision about belief in God and then take personal responsibility for my actions within that decision. In trying to have the best knowledge possible, along with some concern for others, and a bit of a Christian outlook—along with some admittedly questionable personal motives and desires—I use my best judgment. Sometimes the actions are right, sometimes they are wrong. I do not always do the best I know, but the best I can. But I can't palm the responsibility off on God . . . good or bad, right or wrong. The responsibility is mine, and I accept it.

God is my friend. I feel that God loves me and cares for me. I trust Him. He gave me some ability and a bit of sense to be me, to make decisions, and do things. He also requires that I assume the responsibility. When I make mistakes and mess things up, He still loves me. And that's enough.

✝ Who and What Is Man?

Nothing is more intriguing than a human personality. There are frightening possibilities of destructive evil and unlimited possibilities of creative good in a human being. And history has illustrations of both.

However one interprets how man came into being—whether by an instantaneous fiat of creation, or as the result of some sustained ongoing process of creation—humanity, humankind, *man* is the climax of the entire process. And however it was done, God is behind it all.

To believe in God is to believe in *man*, using the generic term, or humanity, if that is preferable. If it helps, I can say that I believe in "male and female." That's the way the writer of Genesis describes Creation:

> So God created man in his own image, in the image of God he created him; male and female created he them.
> . . . And God saw every thing that he had made, and, behold, *it was very good.*
> —Genesis 1:27, 31 (emphasis added)

And the "good" of Creation includes man. I believe in "the original goodness" of man.

Such a belief requires me to say that I am a humanist. A person can be a humanist without believing in God or being a Christian. But how can a Christian be anything other than a humanist. So call me a "Theistic Humanist" or a "Christian Humanist."

But what happened to the original goodness? God took a risk and gave man the freedom of choice. And man botched it! When confronted with the acceptable "tree of life" and the forbidden "tree of the knowledge of good and evil," man chose the latter. We don't know why the knowledge of good and evil was forbidden. If God had limited the choice only to good, then we would not be free. To be human is to be free to choose. No other creature has that capacity. If man is truly free, then he is free to choose the bad as well as the good. In turn he must accept the responsibility for his choices. The evidence of so many wrong choices makes the risk not look so good. But I'm glad God took the risk. Obviously, God still considers the risk worth taking. We are still free to choose. And that is good. We marvel at Shakespeare's insight:

> What a piece of work is man! How noble in reason! How infinite in faculties! In form and moving how express and admirable! In action how like an angel! In apprehension how like a God! . . . —*Hamlet* 2.2.315ff.

But how many know, or believe, the biblical description:

> . . . what is man, that you think of him;
> mere man, that you care for him?
> Yet you made him inferior only to yourself;
> you crowned him with glory and honor.
> You appointed him ruler over everything you made;
> you placed him over all creation. . . . —Psalm 8:4-6 TEV

Read the words again, "inferior only to yourself." The King James Version says "a little lower than the angels," and the Revised Standard Version reads "little less than God." That is a high concept of man. Unfortunately, not all of us see ourselves that way. When we have a low estimate of ourselves, we also diminish God. And that causes us to do dreadful things to ourselves and others.

Suicide is the ultimate way some handle low self-esteem; murder is the way others show no regard for human life. Who knows why they do it. If we read the left-behind notes we may find a clue. Take this one, for example:

> I'm not really needed. Nobody gives a damn for me. I'm just a peanut in the Superdome. I'll step on myself once and for all.

Have any of us ever felt that way about ourselves? If so, we would do well to read the emotional directness in Edna St. Vincent Millay's poem "The Suicide," which begins,

> Curse thee, Life, I will live with thee no more!
> Thou hast mocked me, starved me, beat my body sore![1]

The man then takes his life and finds himself in heaven. He constantly complains about the other angels going to and fro, having things to do, always busy, while he does nothing but sit around all the time. Finally, God speaks to him: "Thou hast had thy task, and laidst it by."

---

[1]From Millay's *Renascence and Other Poems* (New York and London: Harper & Brothers, 1917) 30, as reprinted in *Collected Poems: Edna St. Vincent Millay*, ed. Norma Millay (New York: Harper & Brothers, 1956) 25.

One time a little boy, a victim of domestic tragedy, forced to live in an orphanage or foster homes, feeling desperately miserable, alone, unwanted, and unloved, said, "I just ain't nobody's nothing."

Just so, many people look upon themselves as having no worth or purpose. Such persons are positioned for defeat early on and are halfway there, giving up the struggle before they really begin.

At the other end of life's spectrum, this feeling is particularly true among the aged, especially those who are residents of nursing homes. I am familiar with that feeling, for I have made many visits to such people. My first mother-in-law died at age eighty-four. For eight years she had been a resident of the Ryburn Home in Dallas, a first-class institution. She had no desire to live. When her husband of more than a half century died, she also wanted to die. When her only child, my wife, died, she saw no more reason to live. She felt useless and wanted to die but could not.

An even deeper appreciation for the feeling came when my ninety-four-year-old grandfather (the only father I ever knew) came to live with us. He was mentally alert but physically enfeebled and had lost his independence, no longer able to do for himself. He felt himself to be a burden on everyone, and he wanted to lift that burden.

Someplace in between the suicide, the lad who felt he was "nobody's nothing" and the elderly who feel themselves to be useless burdens, there is something else: a proper estimate of one's self-worth.

The Christian faith is generally interpreted in terms of what to think about God and Jesus Christ. In the natural order of things and in the biblical story, man is on the scene for a long time before we get to Jesus. To start with God and jump to Jesus is to leave out a matter with which the Bible is deeply concerned, namely, what to think about *man*. With that question the Bible constantly confronts us. For now, let us limit ourselves to the New Testament. To be sure, the New Testament (as does the entire Bible) tells us that we are sinners. But hear what Paul says to the Thessalonians:

> You are all children of light. . . .   —1 Thes. 5:5 NRSV

And to the Galatians:

> And because you are sons, God hath sent forth the Spirit of his Son into your hearts. . . .   —Gal. 4:6

And to the Corinthians (a "sure-nuff" bunch of sinners):

> Know ye not that ye are the temple of God. . . .
>   —1 Cor. 3:16

And to the Romans:

> The Spirit itself beareth witness with our spirit, that we are the children of God.   —Rom. 8:16

And such glowing descriptions are confirmed by John:

> Beloved, now are we the sons of God, and it doth not yet appear what we shall be. . . .   —1 John 3:2

We speak of the difficulty of believing in God. I believe in God. There is more difficulty in believing the biblical estimate of humankind. But I believe that also.

The cynic said, "Man is a small but boistrous bit of organic scum that for the time being coats a part of one small planet." I do *not* believe that. Instead, I believe,

> So God created man in his own image. . . . and [God] breathed into his nostrils the breath of life; and man became a living soul. . . . And God saw every thing that he had made, and, behold, it was very good.
>   —Genesis 1:27; 2:7; 1:31

We cannot lightly brush off the lessons we have learned about human behavior. There is something endemically wrong with us from which we need to be cured. Only what the New Testament calls the grace of God can do us any good. The word about sin in the New Testament is the penultimate, not the ultimate word of God's grace in Jesus Christ, a grace that provides resources we cannot provide for ourselves.

I have never been able to believe in that doctrine called Total Depravity. That would mean that man is not worth saving. God did not allow Jesus to die for something totally worthless. Something in man is worth saving, else Jesus would not have died in man's behalf.

So here we stand, confronting man's sin. Yet the New Testament tells us that something else is true about man. Something even more profound than man's sin. Augustine put more stress on human depravity than perhaps any other theologian. What he said has colored our thinking for 1,500 years. But even Augustine—as I recall—said, "Dig deep enough in any man and you will find something divine." I do believe that!

Consider first that this emphasis goes back to Jesus and his way of dealing with individual men and women. Jesus was no sentimentalist about people. He could blaze with indignation about the human situation. He once said that some men deserved to have stones hung about their necks and be cast into the depths of the sea. He knew the offenses of man.

But always beneath Jesus' realistic appraisal of man's perversity was his faith in man. Something divine was there, if he could only get at it and open the way for God's love and grace to release it. A spark of the divine was there, and he was to fan it into a flame.

Facing a woman taken in adultery, condemned by the Law to be stoned as a guilty sinner, Jesus stood alone with her and appealed to something deeper than her sinfulness, something which her accusers did not believe was there. But he knew it was there, and he had to reach it. What a conversation that must have been. Then he told her, "Neither do I condemn you; go, and do not sin again" (John 8:11).

And she had not even asked him for forgiveness, unless it was during the conversation we know nothing about. Beneath our worst, Jesus never doubts the presence of that inner light that lights every person.

Isn't this the deepest truth about us? We are sinners, but we know we are. There is a judgment seat within us, a voice within, distinguishing right and wrong; a divine discontent, condemning the evil and lighting the darkness. That is the most profound fact about us.

A modern cardiovascular surgeon may say that "Man is an ingenious system of portable plumbing." And we are that—with spare parts already built-in. Those of us who have experienced bypass surgery know that. A vein from my leg (a spare part that's not really needed) was used to replace a clogged artery. The mammary artery was rerouted to clear up another blockage.

But "portable plumbing" isn't all that we are. We are souls with dignity, value, and potential usefulness . That surgeon had to learn how to redirect the plumbing. If we dig deep enough, we can find something that is divine. That is the mystery of man. To face what we really are and can become is the most determining factor in a person's life.

Remember Jesus' description of the Prodigal in that far country: "When he came to *himself*." Something inside him did not belong there. Something was not content with his condition. Something in him was not at home among swine. When he came to himself, *his real self*, he arose and left to go home. That was Jesus' undiscourageable insight into human nature.

Consider a second thing. The emphasis on man's dignity and possibility goes back not only to Jesus' attitude toward others, but to what he was himself.

We stress the idea that Jesus was the revelation of God. But let's not overlook the other side: Jesus was also the revelation of man. He shared our human nature, "tempted as we are." So that is what humanity is at its best—*Christlike.* If we could see that Jesus is the revelation of man, it would meet a deep need in all of us.

Ours is a day in which it is easy to take a dim veiw of human nature. The grim facts about human evil are as foreboding as any pessimist would desire. One disillusionment after another has crashed down upon us, until human wickedness threatens the very survival of the earth itself and of the human race. The news media flood us daily with stories of our meanness and corruption. The pictures of daily human conduct—from dirty politics to the horrors of war, from prison riots to murder on the streets—cause us to see the crassness and coarseness of human nature.

Then comes the New Testament, crying out for the world to hear and see that Jesus is also man. What is more, as one of the early Christians put it,

> [Christ became what we are that we might become what he is], until we all attain . . . to mature manhood, to the measure of the stature of the fulness of Christ.
> —Ephesians 4:13

Does that sound downright incredible? Of course it does. For the most part, it is easier to accept the Christian idea of God than it is to accept the Christian idea of man. Being made in the image of God, to be Christlike is to be oneself fulfilled, brought to maturity.

Gutzon Borglum, the sculptor, was once working on a head of Abraham Lincoln. Each day he chipped away the stone, and each day a cleaning woman swept up the chips. Amazed, she watched the head of Lincoln emerge under the

artist's hands until at last, when the work was almost finished, she exclaimed, "Mr. Borglum, how'd you know Mr.
Lincoln was in that stone?"

The emergence of great character from the rough rock
of our unshaped lives often seems utterly improbable. But
Christain faith has been insistent: Mr. Lincoln is in that
stone; Christlike character is in our lives.

This, then, is the practical consequence of the matter:
to identify ourselves with our best self, not the worst. And
it is our choice. The worst is there. We know it only too well;
so does everyone else, because it can't be hidden. Any psychiatrist knows the hidden dark side. But let's not call *that*
our real self. Potential Christlikeness is in us too.

Life can be a bad bargain. Yet, as Christians, we are determined to strive to make it worthwhile. To do this requires courage, courage to see life as it is and yet persist in
living as it could be. This requires the courage to be oneself.

David Viscott, author of the recently much-discussed
How to Live with Another Person, talks about the courage to
be oneself. About the Yiddish word "mensch" he says,

> A mensch is a person who can feel affection toward an-
> other man, who doesn't feel threatened by anything he
> thinks or feels, learns from his mistakes, doesn't need to
> pull you down in order to pull himself up.[2]

A real person, then, is one who knows who he or she is,
what the limitations are, and yet strives not to be someone
else, but uses whatever is available to him or her to the fullest extent.

If we are concerned only with the day-to-day things we
are likely to be pessimistic. If we have visions of something

---

[2]As quoted in *The Times-Picayune* (New Orleans), 6
March 1975, 7:6.

better, we tend to be optimistic. Some people regard optimism as a kind of foolish naiveté. Not so! If we are sensitive and disturbed by life's ugliness but still retain the hope that things in the world could be better, some people think that this is an escape from reality. It is not!

We are aware that a lot is wrong with the human condition, with the way people act toward one another. But to dwell on that and on nothing else can be paralyzing, self-defeating. Why not see if there is anything we can do to improve matters. If everything were perfect, there would be no challenge, no hope for improvement. Life is never quite so good as one hopes it to be, nor is it quite so bad as some fear it to be.

I've seen lives transformed. Some lives have so long identified with the worst that they actually believe themselves to be scum. And they act like it. Then a new insight comes.
Someone tells them that God is mindful of them.
Someone tells them that Jesus Christ believes in them.
Someone tells them what they can become.
And they begin to believe that!

Conversion isn't talked about much these days, and sudden conversion is almost totally neglected. Not many of us see it at all. In fact, some decry it altogether as being an old-fashioned concept. A recent book on psychology used the term "instantaneous reorientation." That psychologist may never have said "sudden conversion," but instantaneous reorientation was all right. He had seen that happen. So have I. Call it what you will, changes can happen, even suddenly.

> But when he came to himself he said, . . . "I will arise
> and go to my father."   —Luke 15:17-18

We need this message. The world is in a mess. Individual lives are torn to shreds. This is a chaotic, frightening and frightened world. This is not the first time humanity has faced perplexity and dismay. It began with the expulsion of Adam and Eve from Eden. At the same time, God began working on a way back.

A century and a half ago, the dying Duke of Wellington is said to have remarked, "I thank God that I shall be spared from seeing the consummation of ruin that is gathering about us." Why, even the British Empire rose to its greatest heights after that. If we are ever tempted to such pessimism, remember, doors of opportunity are open to us which were not even here twenty-five years ago. And there are many doors yet to be opened.

To see our world in its desperate condition, one is almost scared to death of what could happen. But remember what the hymn writer said: "This is my Father's world."

Don't read the headlines only; read the "Good News" too. Yes, I believe in man:

Made in the image of God . . . fearfully and wonderfully made . . . a little lower than the angels—inferior only to God . . . children of God . . . sons of light . . . and it is not yet made manifest what we shall be.

✝ Sin? . . . What's That?

André Gide, the French novelist, in his short story "The Pastoral Symphony," tells of a young woman who was blind from birth. Her blindness so sheltered her that she had a childish, sentimental picture of people, which neither her family nor friends tried to upset. Then one day an operation made it possible for her to see. Two things struck her with great force:

Nature was more beautiful than she had imagined.
The faces of people were sadder than she had expected.

She almost wished that her eyes had not been made to see.

This sad aspect of people's faces is something all of us must consider.

In the beginning God created . . . man. And God said that all He had created was good. Man was to be happy and enjoy all that God had created. Then something happened. We call what happened *sin*. When we try to define sin (evil) and pinpoint its origin, we have problems. The best explanation of the orgin of sin/evil is given to us by the writer of Genesis. But even that explanation leaves us much room to speculate. And we have.

I once saw a clever, one-panel, wordless cartoon. The scene was a garden with a man and a woman standing among some trees and behind a hedge. In front of the hedge was a little wagon drawn by a snake. In the wagon was an apple. On the side of the wagon was a sign, saying WEL-COME WAGON.

There is a story told about a theology professor who was lecturing on the problem of evil. He paused and said, "Mr. Jones, could you tell us the origin of evil?" (Why is it no one ever asks about the origin of *good*?)

The student, who had been dozing, was startled into consciousness and, not having heard the question, said, "Professor, I used to know, but I've forgotten."

The professor paused, then in awed tones said, "Class, this is a momentous occasion. In the history of the universe only two persons have known the answer to the origin of evil: God, and he never told us, and your fellow student, who has forgotten."

I believe in sin. However, I have never been able to accept the idea of the "total depravity" of man, or the usual explanations of "original sin." If everything God created was good, including man, I had rather emphasize the "original goodness" of man. If we are worthless, why should God go to such lengths to get us back? A king does not stoop to pick up a copper penny. Nor would God send Jesus to die for man unless man is worth saving. Something in us—call it the image of God or whatever—has value.

Still, there is the fact of human sin/evil. However the original image became defaced or the goodness perverted, and whatever it is that causes generation after generation to "come short of the glory of God," the facts of life show that systemic evil is a part of human life. It is sin that causes the sad aspect in people's faces.

Sin is never a pleasant thing to talk about. Despite what some may think, most preachers do not enjoy pointing out the devastating fact of sin. Some preachers, however, do seem to get a vicarious thrill in talking about some specific sins, especially sexual ones. That makes me suspicious, for that may be that preacher's weakness. There are some folk who would prefer that the preacher never mention sin. A lady once said, "After all, why talk about sin to so many nice people?"

There was a college in the South that advertised its campus as being "seven miles from known sin." But that same college had fences around its campus, with guards at the entrances, and the most rigid set of rules imaginable.

Many think we are nice people, sin is out there at a comfortable distance of "seven miles," being done by someone else.

But no matter how much we try to evade, the fact of sin remains. Just take a look at any newspaper or watch the television news. See the sadness in people's faces as you walk the street. No, not all sadness is caused by sin. There is something about our life which, if we are at all sensitive, should cause us to take seriously this thing called sin. We may not like what we see, but once our eyes are opened, we must admit that modern man has a great deal of sadness in his face. Something is wrong. Life was not meant to be sad.

In earlier days some in the church went overboard in stressing the idea that man was totally depraved, a hopelessly worthless, sinful creature. Then in the first third of this century, we had just the opposite. Give him enough education, the right environment, and enough time and man would produce a utopia. Both views have proved to be inadequate. Yet each has a measure of truth. Somewhere in between is a better truth about man.

None of us wants to be gloomy or morbid and dwell on the negative side of things. We are quite aware that some things that have been called sin are not that at all. Some theologians and preachers, in emphasizing the evils of human nature, have sometimes exaggerated and distorted the picture.

But we cannot ignore the facts of the world in which we live. We are in for a rude awakening if, reacting against the exaggeration, we get lopsided in the other direction by trying to ignore or modify the tragic reality of sin.

In our efforts to emphasize the positive elements of man's nature we must not be Pollyannaish about his negative side. If the idea of sin has faded out of modern man's mind, it does not mean that he is getting too intelligent to accept it. Rather, it could mean that he is getting too morally insensitive to discern it.

Every generation produces those who, disregarding facts, spin fascinating theories about "the nothingness of evil." In our day there are two groups who give a lot of attention to glossing over the fact of sin. Each has many followers who are good people. Such an attitude just does not measure up to the facts of life which we observe every day. Despite the allure of such theories, I think it is more realistic to follow the teachings of the Bible, particularly the New Testament. Those writers were experts in the field of human behavior. There are two questions we need to ask as we read the New Testament: What do the New Testament writers say? Does what they say correspond to what we know?

When we read the New Testament (or Genesis 1–3) we find no explanation of the origin of evil/sin. Those writers took the existence of sin for granted, even as they assumed the fact of God and their own existence.

Sin is a moral twist in life, something endemic, they

say. It is something in life that ought not to be. It is a downward bent in human nature that disorganizes life and sets up discord in the world. But let's not have them say that sin in man is inherited. The principle of sin is as universal as life itself. But we become personally guilty when we personally sin. We are not born guilty of sin.

Read just two sentences from the New Testament. These are not isolated proof texts; they are summaries of central truth.

> All have sinned, and come short of the glory of God.
> —Romans 3:23

> If any man says he has not sinned, he lies; he deceives himself and the truth is not in him. —1 John 1:9

The New Testament writers never tone down the fact of sin. They never soften it with explanations of extenuating circumstances. They do not call sin a mistake in judgment, the absence of light, nor a blunder. They call it sin, something of which every person is guilty, and from which every person must be delivered and forgiven. Or, refusing the grace of God's forgiveness, they reflect the aspect of sadness in being away from Eden.

It does not matter whether the New Testament view be optimistic or pessimistic, modern or obsolete, popular or unpopular. The only question is, *Is it true?* What are the facts as we know them? Such an approach ought to appeal to our pragmatic minds.

Suppose we forget theology and sermons. Let's just look at human life as we know it. Take a walk down the street, any street. What does what we find there teach us? There are thousands of people who have never read the New Testament, who haven't the foggiest notion of what it teaches about sin. But in their everyday relationships they live and move and have their being on the assumption of the reality of the existence of evil.

Ask a banker for a loan and right off he starts thinking about the sin question. He may know nothing of the origin of evil, but he knows how to call up a credit rating.

Apply for some life insurance, and the company has some pertinent questions to ask at this point.

On the corner is a policemen. Who is he? What is he doing there? He is a silent witness to the reality of sin.

Why do we lock our cars and put the keys in our pockets? Automobile makers are not theologically trained. They may not have read the Bible. But they are theologically conditioned, and they have read human beings. They are under no illusions about the facts of daily life.

It's all very well in our sheltered rooms to talk about "the nothingness of evil" or "the absence of light." But in the world of reality such theories are no good. Out in the world we must be realistic. Out there we are biblical believers accepting the verdict of those writers about the reality of sin. Sin is no ghost that preachers have conjured up. It is no mere creation of minds made morbid by the fear of God. Sin is a realistic fact with which humanity is compelled to deal.

Suppose we come closer and take a look at ourselves. It is an amazing thing that we should ever debate about sin, since we all have so much inside information on the subject. I may think I know more about it than you do. And you may think you know more about it than I do. Each of us has more trouble with ourselves than we do with anyone else. Paul spoke for everyone:

For the good that I would, I do not;
but the evil which I would not, that I do.
. . . wretched man that I am.   —Romans 7:19, 24

Ian Maclaren has an old story about Andrew Harris who was nominated as an elder in a Scottish village church.

The night came to hear objections and the moderator called out, "Andrew Harris! Is there any reason he should not be elected an elder in the kirk?"

No one arose, for all believed in Andrew Harris. They knew him. But Andrew himself arose and said,

> My friends, there is a man in this city of whom I am deeply envious, and wherefore because I am a true witness against the life of Andrew Harris, I now object and declare he is not fit to be an elder in the kirk.

Most of us would not be that honest. At least we seldom admit what is hidden in the deep inner places of ourselves. If we did, none of us would be pastors or deacons/elders or anything else. We know what's there. Everyone who understands himself and is honest with himself is a true witness of this point. We wouldn't elect each other if we knew everything. It is good that we do not know. We don't need to know everything about each other. We all need some privacy. We live with what we are. We try to understand that we are all sinners. Then we try a little harder to be a bit better. And we should then be more understanding of others.

I have never met anyone who said what a man said to Jesus one day, "I have kept the commandments since my youth" (Luke 18:21). Nor have you. We all have broken some of those commandments.

> For I do not do the good I want,
> but the evil I do not want is what I do. —Romans 7:19

That isn't just one man's ancient confession. That is honest testimony echoing the inner life of everyone of us. We need no book or person to tell us that. We know when we defy God. We know when we take the low road instead of the high. We know when an impure thought leads to an unclean act that leaves a soiled life. We know how mixed in motives even our best intentions are.

Sin, in the Christian sense, centers in the ego, the motivating self. It is more than mere conduct. Since God is holy and righteous, anything that opposes God is sin. The Bible uses various terms to describe sin: trespass, transgress, miss the mark, selfishness, love of the world, coming short of the glory of God, rebellion against God, that is, living contrary to God's purposes for us. No one escapes it.

I know what sin is but have difficulty defining it. Some of the things we call sins are social conventions. To drink alcohol is for some Christians a sin, for others is is not. Even the biblical writers had difficulty defining sin. They used different words in Hebrew and Greek which we lump together in one English word—sin. But they were in agreement that sin had to do with rebellion against God, deviation from God, and wrongdoing toward our fellow man. As good a summary as we can find is in Paul's statement that "all have sinned [missed the mark], and come short of the glory of God" (Romans 3:23).

To come short of the glory of God and the dignity that God intends for us is to sin. If all God created is good, including man, then sin is a perversion of that good. The sex drive is good, until we pervert it in debauched behavior. Ambition is good, until we distort it by crushing each other in order to achieve our ambitions. All of what are called "the seven deadly sins"—pride, coveteousness, lust, anger, envy, gluttony, and sloth—are corruptions of things that are not evil in themselves. When we deface the image of God that is in us all, we sin. As my friend Will Campbell puts it, "We are all bastards. But God loves us anyway."

What is sin? We know what it is! We know that it is what we have done in deviation from God. More than that, we know what James meant in his epistle when he said,

Whoever knows what is right to do and fails to do it, for
him it is sin.   —James 4:17

So, sin is both evil done and good left undone.

Marguerite Wilkinson has a bit of verse entitled
"Guilty":

> I never cut my neighbor's throat,
>   My neighbor's purse I never stole;
> I never spoiled his house and land;
>   But God have mercy on my soul.
>
> For I am haunted night and day
>   By all the deeds I have not done,
> The unattempted loveliness,
>   Or costly valor, never won.

With all of our hopes and all our efforts to achieve
something better, we are up against a powerful adversary.
There is something tragic and terrible in human nature that
takes our best qualities and our finest efforts and turns them
into failure. We need a rediscovery of what past generations called *sin*. If we have a better name for it, let's use it.
But let's also recognize the reality of it. That is the key to
our understanding of something fascinating and far-reach-
ing that is happening in our time.

If what our fathers called sin seems vague and unreal,
even old-fashioned to our generation, it is not because sin
has lessened. It is mostly because we have been calling it
by other names. A new science has been born in our day.
We call it psychology, "the study of the soul." We have
found some new labels for old evils, a whole new vocabu-
lary for what in former years we were content to call sin.
Substitute the word *complex* for sin, *frustration* for conviction, *neurosis* or *morbid fear* for what in less enlightened days
was known as demon possession, and the old devils are
back with us, dressed in the latest fashions and baptized

with a new name. Nevertheless, the former terms described people then, and they describe them now.

At first this new science was viewed with suspicion by clergymen who always seem to fear anything new. To be sure, some psychologists and psychiatrists did not, and do not now, believe in God. (It has always seemed a bit strange to me that those engaged in "the study of the soul" can say, "There is no soul.") Nowadays such unbelief is becoming a bit more rare. More and more men of psychology and theology are working together. Far from denying the New Testament, modern psychology is bringing light and confirmation to its basic teachings. Go down with Freud into the lower depths of what he called the subconscious (id), examine what goes on in that dark cellar of concealment, and you will get a whiff of depravity that not even John Calvin could dream up.

Far more real than we realize, the penalties, judgments, and retributions are not waiting for some far-off Judgment Day; in personal lives they are right now taking their toll. Today volumes are being written fortifying the New Testament message which speaks of "the hidden things . . . of the heart" (1 Corthinthians 4:5):

The effects of guilt on personality.

The seeping poison of self-centered living.

How hatred can wreck physical health.

People who might never hear about sin from a pulpit are hearing it from the psychiatrist's couch. They are being told they need to get that buried stuff of life out of the dark, bring it to the surface, ventilate it, face it, and get rid of it, as one gets rid of garbage.

What's so new about that? Nothing, really. That is precisely what the New Testament teaches. It is exactly what Christian churches have been saying for almost 2,000 years. Or is it? It is at this point that we must ask some questions. But can we deal with sin as a "soul sickness" only, or heal a wounded conscience as an orthopedist straightens a twisted bone? Or is there some missing element in our modern therapy?

I think it was William Hocking who once said, "The secular psychiatrist all too often undertakes a work which, purely as a psychiatrist, he can't finish." What did he mean by that? Something we find the Psalmist saying, "Against thee, thee only, have I sinned" (Psalm 51:4). Against thee, O God, we have sinned!

The New Testament tells us the story of a cross. We have made that cross the symbol of our faith. We do not see sin in its true light until we see it there, set against the background of a love that suffered because of sin. Perhaps the psychiatrist can look impersonally at our sin. But there is a "depth psychology" that is deeper than such objective probings. Our sin is not only against ourselves, our health, our welfare: it is sin against God, too! God, the loving Heavenly Father who suffers at home while we sin in far countries.

The cross is the central meeting point of the mystery and meaning of life. The cross is the assurance that somehow God is present with us in the midst of the human struggle. And no man's sin is done with until he faces up to that cross.

Let's look at it this way. Is that drunken fellow staggering and reeling down the street comedy or tragedy? If you are talking about my father or son, I would know, just as you would know if it were your loved one. You see, love makes the difference in how we measure sin. All around us are the tragedies of life:

Broken, shattered lives.

Fragmented homes and orphaned children.

Deserting husbands and faithless wives.

Alienated youth.

These are the events of life. Novelists write their stories in books. Newspapers and television announce the scandals in lurid headlines. Hollywood works it all up into an attractive performance.

From a distance all this may be viewed quite casually. From the perspective of a spectator, it does not seem like sin at all. But let it walk into your front door. Let the man— husband or son—become coarse, cheap, and crude. Let the woman in the scandal be your wife or daughter. Let the drug seller or addict be your child. Let sin lay hold on someone dear to you. Let the knife stick into your heart. Sin loses its glamor then. Through the eyes of love and love alone do we see what sin really is? We are close to the mightiest truth ever let loose among us: "There was a lad who left home and broke his father's heart." And in a few terse sentences Jesus told a story (Luke 15:11-32).

It is the story of EVERYMAN, as the early church called it. Such a common story, so familiar, so often repeated, so close to home, so near to where we live. We can fill in the details easily enough from our own experiences: the wrong crowd, the wrong ideals, the wrong choices, and misused freedom . . . *the story of everyman*.

But that's not all. Look back home. There is "The Waiting Father." Sin had walked into that home. The man went on about his work. He worked too hard and too long, his neighbors said. The servants couldn't stand the look of sadness in his eyes. The grey in his hair became more noticeable. The lines in his face were more deeply etched. Friends tried to get him to take it easy. For his own health's sake he must not take it so hard, they said. "Yes, I know," he said. "I know other boys have gone wrong, some far worse. But to think that my Absalom, *my son, Absalom!* . . . "

The nearer we get to the heart of God, the broken heart of God the Father, the clearer we see sin for what it is and understand why there was a cross upon a green hill outside a city wall.

Once a man who described himself as a lapsed agnostic chanced into an Episcopal church where he heard the Prayer of General Confession:

> We have erred and strayed from Thy ways like lost sheep. We have followed too much the devices and desires of our own hearts. . . . We have left undone those things which we ought to have done; and we have done those things which we ought not to have done.

"That's my kind of people," he said. "At last, a church I can belong to!"

I believe that.

> If we confess our sins, he is faithful and just, and will forgive our sins. . . .   —1 John 1:9

I believe that, too.

✝ View of the Bible

When we open a Bible the first thing we read is something like this:

The Holy Bible. Revised Standard Version, Containing the Old and New Testaments, Translated from the Original Tongues, Being the Version Set Forth A.D. 1611, Revised A.D. 1881–1885 and A.D. 1901, Compared with the Most Ancient Authorities and Revised A.D. 1946–1952.[1]

This is an impressive statement. It breathes of romance and intrigue, suggesting far-off exotic Eastern lands, and conjures up visions of men and women and the man-

---

[1]This typical definitive title is that of the Revised Standard Version (New York: Thomas Nelson & Sons, N.T. 1946, O.T. 1952).

ners and customs of strange, ancient times. There is also the reminder of the loving care and meticulous preservation of the texts of those "most ancient authorities."

Were I to say at the outset, "I believe the Bible from cover to cover," some would turn me off, saying, "That's ridiculous!" Were I to say, "Some of the things between the covers I do not believe," some would turn me out, saying, "That's blasphemy!" How am I to get it across that there is a place for belief someplace in between? I *do* believe the Bible, but not everything between its covers.

The story of the Bible and how we got it is as fascinating as anything in historical or fictional literature. What a historical novelist like Irwin Stone or James Michener could do with that story!

Why bother with a book that was put together some 2,000 years ago? (We might as well ask why read Socrates or Plato.) Should we not be more interested in what's going on today? Of course we should want to know what is going on now. And being interested in today we need to know something about yesterday. The Bible is about *today*. It has a classic timeless quality.

The Bible is not just another book with a lot of interesting things about God in it. It is a book about people, people who found God coming alive and becoming real to them, sometimes in surprising ways, and demanding that they do something about Him. God does not figure in the Bible as a subject of debate. Rather than being argued, God is assumed. God is regarded as the unconditional reality who is thoroughly personal, the souce of all natural and personal life.

There are those who say that the Bible is a recording of man's search for God; that it is a record of the slow, agonizing quest from primitive origins to a highly sophisticated monotheism. It is that. But it is more. The thing that most distinguishes God in the Bible is His entering into relations with man. We may be closer to the truth when we say the Bible is the record of God's search for man. Although primitive records suggest some belief in deity—gods of one kind or another—people seem more prone to try to escape from God than to find Him. In spite of this, in the Bible God continues to seek after those same people, refusing to give them up, despite their countless evasions and continued rebuffs.

But there is more than that. The Bible not only tells how God sought people in the past, it is also a means by which God seeks us out today. We just can't read the Bible without getting involved. Why? Because the nature and experiences of those biblical people are basically the same as ours. Because the questions we ask were their questions also: What is the meaning of life? Does it make any difference to believe in God? Is Jesus any more than just a great man? Why does life so often seem futile and purposeless? Why be good when the good suffer and the evil prosper? Why is there such a thing as evil? Is there really life after death?Those same questions are asked in the Bible, with the same search for answers. We have no more satisfactorily ultimate answers to the mysteries of human life than did our ancestors. Nor can we explain human conflict—the comedy/tragedy, the glory/disappointment—any better than they.

It takes some courage to honestly ask such questions. And to the extent that we ask them we find ourselves involved in what goes on in the Bible. The Bible does not hand out easy answers to us. It tells us how people hammered out some answers for themselves out of their daily experiences.

The Bible is a record of human perceptions of God's acting in the lives of men and women. As we read it, the possibility is opened up that God can speak through those lives and events to us. The Bible is a certified letter with our name and address on it. It is more than a historical document: it is an urgent invitation with an R.S.V.P.

The word "bible" is equivalent to the Greek word βιβλία *biblia* that comes from βίβλος *biblos*, which at first meant the inner bark of the papyrus plant. The word came to mean that part of the papyrus from which a paper-like writing substance was made. Eventually, writings on this "paper" were called *biblia*, books. (The Greek translation of Daniel 9:2 refers to the writings of the prophets as τὰ βιβλία, "the books.") Through Latin, this Greek term came into English as "bible." So, our Bible became known as "the books" and then as *The Book*.

This large collection of books, sixty-six in all, was written by at least forty writers during a long period of more than 1,500 years. With the exception of Luke, the writers were probably all Hebrews and Jews. The Hebrew Bible or Old Testament was written in Hebrew with a smattering of Aramaic; the New Testament was written in Greek. For most of the English-speaking world, the Bible is the Authorized (King James) Version, first published in A.D. 1611. More and better translations today offer better understanding.

We must remember that for the greater part of the time that separates us from the time when the books of the Bible were written, *every* copy had to be copied by hand. Printing was invented in Europe about 1450. The Hebrew Old Testament first appeared in print around 1488. Erasmus's Greek New Testament came about twenty-eight years later, in 1516. Prior to that time there were only *manuscripts*, handwritten copies. It is virtually impossible to copy great quantities of writing without making mistakes (not even excellent typists can do that, including those who do their work with computer word processors). Furthermore, some copyists were not always particular about exact accuracy, and editors sometimes deliberately altered what they thought was in error or obscure. Thus no two manuscripts were ever exactly alike. So it is absolutely impossible for us to have a copy of the Bible in its exact original form. And it is rather foolish to speculate or talk about how it might have been in the original.

As late as 1947, the earliest known Hebrew manuscript of any part of the Bible could be dated no earlier than the ninth century after Christ. The discovery of the Dead Sea Scrolls during 1947–1956 gave us manuscript portions of every book of the Old Testament except Esther. Most are fragments, but there was a virtually complete scroll of Isaiah. These manuscripts have been dated paleographically as early as the second century B.C. This means we now have Old Testament manuscripts that are at least 1,000 years older than we had in 1947. Who knows what archeologists will find tomorrow?

Now, let's take a look at some of those "most ancient authorities" and see how we got the Bible.

During the third century B.C., when the Jews were dispersing throughout the Greek-speaking world, they began habitually to speak Greek. Their native Hebrew language was becoming unknown. The need arose for a Greek translation of their scriptures. Such a translation was made in Alexandria, Egypt, where Jews were numerous, interest in literature was lively, and scholars were available. This translation is known as the "Septuagint," or "the work of the seventy," from the supposed number of translators who worked on it. Tradition says the Septuagint was completed by "seventy-two scholars in seventy-two days."

After the destruction of Jerusalem in A.D. 70, the Jewish leaders, deprived of their national identity and threatened by the spread of many sects (including Christianity), were forced to make their sacred books the center of their national unity. They felt it necessary to define authoritatively which books were to be regarded as sacred, and to secure, as far as possible, the purity of the texts of those books. Between the years A.D. 90 and 100—at the so-called Council of Jamnia—a synod of Jews ratified existing custom and selected the thirty-nine books we have in the Old Testament today. They did not include what we call the Apocrypha, and no more writings were to be added. Rigid requirements for accurate copying of the texts were established. We can be sure that the Old Testament as we know it is, as nearly as humanly possible, without material change since about A.D. 100.

The New Testament is a different story. For some twenty or thirty years after Jesus' death, the story of his life and his teachings were circulated orally by the preaching and teaching of the disciples. Then Paul began writing his letters. Paul had no idea he was writing "sacred scripture." His letters were to help churches, groups of Christians, to deal with specific problems. Some time later the Synoptic Gospels (Matthew, Mark, and Luke) and the Acts of the Apostles appeared. The Gospel of John and the Revelation probably came late during the first century.

An early Christian named Marcion (about A.D. 85–160) decided that the Old Testament and the New Testament were about two different Gods, so he excluded the entire Old Testament. For his New Testament he included only Luke and ten of Paul's letters which he considered "safe."

Because of such antics as Marcion's, the early church began to develop a standard list of authorized writings. This was called the "canon," meaning the norm or standard of measurement of Christian faith. The Old Testament was accepted because it was seen as the preparation for Jesus Christ. Agreement was gradually reached as to which of the many Christian writings should be approved. By A.D. 200 there was general agreement about the Gospels, Acts, and Paul's letters. Other writings were on the border. Of all the books, Revelation had the hardest time making it. As late as the Middle Ages there was doubt regarding its inclusion. But at least by A.D. 367 a list had been approved which contained the twenty-seven books we now have in the New Testament.

Then along came Jerome, who in the year A.D. 405 completed his translation of the Bible into Latin, the "Vulgate." The Latin Vulgte was to have enormous influence on Christianity in the West, in fact on all of Western Civilization. It would be false to say that the New Testament as we have it depended on Jerome or any one individual. However, it is probably true that Jerome finally determined for Western Christianity what books the New Testament would contain. What he gave us is essentially what we have.

However, the war was not over. During the fifteenth and sixteenth centuries some disputes arose. Erasmus, Luther, and Calvin felt some books were of less value and of a lower class. Finally, the Council of Trent (A.D. 1545–1563) declared the final word, final so far as the Roman Catholic Church was concerned. Regarding the Bible, that word was the Old Testament (the thirty-nine books plus the books Catholics call Deuterocanonical and Protestants call Apocrypha) and the twenty-seven New Testament books we now have.

(The story of the translation of the Bible into English is a fascinating story in itself, but now is not the time to tell it.)

Fallible men? Yes. And there were disputes. But they were devout men, too. Of course there was much of the human element in the final selection of the biblical canon. But we have it, and it is rather miraculous that we do.

This means that we have had our Bible in its present form, both the Old and New Testaments, for at least 1,500 years, and almost 450 years since the Council of Trent.

The work of the scholar and the critic has been of great assistance in our understanding of the Bible. Not all criticism is bad, none of it is intended to destroy faith. Rather, biblical criticism is to make our faith more intelligible, and thus more real. The reverent, honest scholar is searching for truth. When that scholar applies the methods of critical study to the Bible, he puts us under an obligation to him, for we are also looking for God's truth. The scholar tries to tell us what the Bible actually said originally, thus our understanding of what it can say to us is increased. The Bible has nothing to fear from honest investigation. Neither does the believer have anything to fear from what is found. No other piece of literature has been subjected to more serious critical scrutiny from both friend and foe than the Bible. Still it stands.

The chief concern of the Old Testament writers was people and their personalities and problems. They were interested in the progress of people to comprehend God and wrote about the ever-enlarging revelation of God to people. The New Testament writers emphasize a message. After the brief "biography" of Jesus in the four Gospels, the other twenty-three books deal with the message of Jesus. Those writers concentrated on how Jesus fitted into the mighty acts of God toward man's redemption. They wanted Jesus to be known as God's fulfillment, the Messiah, the Saviour. The writer of the Epistle to the Hebrews summarized it beautifully:

> In many and various ways God spoke of old to our fathers by the prophets; but in these last days he has spoken to us by a Son.   —Hebrews 1:1-2

To sort out and draw all of this together, let me use the first three chapters of Genesis. The writer of Genesis was not concerned with science as we understand it. He knew nothing of our scientific approach or method. He was not trying to write a detailed account of creation which, centuries later, judged by his methods, would be called correct or incorrect. He was not trying to answer the scientist's *how*. (The science textbooks I studied in college are for the most part hopelessly out-of-date. So are yours, if they were written ten years ago.) The writer of Genesis was not concerned with the scientific. He was concerned with the religious emphasis—the *why*. He was interested in God's part in the universe and man's place in it. The method or process of creation did not bother him. To him, the one vital thing was, "In the beginning God."

We cannot overstate the importance of the first three chapters of Genesis. Critical study has looked at these chapters in a manner not true of any other document ever written. So we have two accounts of creation in these chapters. So we have different names for God, Elohim and Jehovah (or Yahweh, as scholars say). So different men wrote at different times, and a later man put them together. So what?

These three chapters are important because they are the most orderly, consistent, and valid account that we have about the beginning of the world in which we live. More than that, without them we would have no basis for theology. Practically every theological idea can be traced to the Genesis account of creation, temptation, the fall (sin) of man, and the planting of the seed for man's return to God.

This is what the Bible is about: God, man, life, sin, death, and destiny. That is why we read it. That is why we want to know as much as we possibly can know about it.

When we begin to read the Bible we find ourselves in a strange world. At first glance, it is a world totally different from and far removed from anything we know. The thoughts, methods of expression, and concepts seem to be on the primitive side. Our credulity is strained at many places. We read early about a place called the Garden of Eden where God walks, talks, and dines with human beings. There are a lot of family genealogies that bog us down, but which would delight the Daughters of the American Revolution or the Mormons. But, centuries later, these genealogies show up with significance in the New Testament books of Matthew and Luke. Most of the biblical record is the account of one man's family, Abraham of Ur, followed generation after generation. The people of this family came to be known as God's "Chosen People," chosen not for privilege, but for responsibility.

This family is seen as a group of bedouins wandering from Ur to Egypt, then from Egypt across a wilderness to a place called Canaan. The Old Testament tells of their settlement in that land, of their judges and tribes, and of their kings and little kingdoms that were more like pawns in the game of international intrigue played by the great nations of the Middle East.

The Bible is full of common, ordinary, everyday life and people. That's what the writers were interested in—life and people. And they sought to direct the life of the people in the ways of God.

The Bible deals with life's basic issues: God, man, sin, life, death, and destiny. It does not deal with those issues as abstract philosophical ideas, nor does it talk about them in propositions or theories. In the Bible, truth about life is not argued out; it is acted out. Watching these actors on the stage called the Bible, hearing their dialogue, and seeing their actions, we see firsthand the dramatic facts of life, death, and destiny with which everyone of us must deal: selfishness and unselfishness; mean ambitions and magnanimous loyalties; wild passions and difficult self-control; cruelty and gentleness; cowardice and courage; hatred and love. All of these are in the Bible not as topics for academic discussion, but as forces that live and move and work themselves out in an ancient people who startle us by their resemblance to us. If their methods of expression and their concepts are on the primitive side, their emotions and problems are quite on the contemporary side.

Two currently popular words are "realism" and "relevance." This is nothing new. The realism of the Bible is uncompromising and its relevance is as up-to-date as tomorrow's newspaper. There is no effort to gloss over the ugly depths of human meanness, nor to smooth over the heroes. The warts and all are there. The shadows of life are let in, causing the highlights to become more convincing. Humanity is seen against the background of the universe. Even the obscure life is kept from being insignificant because the Bible relates the remotest life to the transcendent fact of God.

The Bible takes existence, which might otherwise be commonplace, and links it with the eternal. We see people struggling, groping, sinning, yet aspiring, lifting their eyes toward God and finding themselves surprisingly nearer to God than they had dared to dream, for God was reaching out toward them. In all this, the Bible is not merely talking *about* life; it grows out of life in an extraordinarily direct and vivid way.

The Bible is rooted in life. All of the crude details, the exquisite poetry, the dramatic episodes are the stuff of life out of which and through which the revelation of God comes. The revelation of God is tied up with the life experiences of individual people and the nation of those people—Israel. The Bible is man's thoughts about God, not God's thoughts about Man. While our creeds and confessions say

> The Bible is the Word of God, or
> The Bible contains the Word of God,

it is also true that the Bible is and contains man's response to that Word. The Bible may be the sphere of the divine encounter, but the place where that encounter takes place is in human life—in people, in a person, in you and me.

All of this implies a far more vital view of the Bible than most of us have. To many the Bible is a fragmentary thing of shreds and patches, a few bright spots here and some high places there, but mostly an unknown and barren wasteland. To most people, knowledge of the Bible consists of something about the first part of Genesis; a few Psalms (23, and perhaps 51 and 139); some Old Testament stories about Joseph, Samson, and David; the Sermon on the Mount—vaguely—and the Golden Rule; the parables about the Prodigal and the Good Samaritan; and perhaps the "Love Chapter" (1 Corinthians 13). Also, John 14 and Psalm 23 are almost always requested for funerals.

But that is not the Bible. That is to mistake the parts for the whole. To give just value to the parts, we need to see the Bible as a whole. In doing so we can see just how relevant the Bible is to life—all of life, *our life.*

Statistics keep telling us the Bible is the world's best-selling book. On the other hand, other statistics tell us that, worldwide, Karl Marx's *Das Kapital* outsells the Bible. For all the Bible sales, experience tells us that it isn't being read, or if it is, we don't know what it says, nor are we practicing what it teaches. The Bible has become what Bruce Barton called it over sixty years ago, *The Book Nobody Knows.*[2]

Throughout the world today there is a spirit of revolt. Almost every cherished tradition is everywhere being questioned. The old empires have fallen apart, and most of the monarchs have been retired from office while other empires and rulers are taking shape. Economic pressures, political events, racial unrest, demands for a larger portion of earth's natural resources, and clamorings for self-determination are bringing revolt and change. The faith of our fathers is in eclipse, and in many cases is being repudiated altogether. Our civilization seems sick unto death, and people in desperation are turning to desperate remedies, so that often the cure is as bad as, or worse than, the disease. Many have ceased to believe that "there is a balm in Gilead." And if they do vaguely remember, they forget that that balm is "to heal the sin-sick soul."

The Bible is the record of God's redemptive activity from beginning to end. In the opening chapters of Genesis we have the Garden of Eden story and man's sin which caused his expulsion. At the end, the Book of Revelation tells the story of another Garden City of God. Paradise Regained is set over against Paradise Lost. If we want to know

---

[2]*The Book Nobody Knows* was the title of Barton's book on the subject (New York: Editions for the Armed Services, 1940).

where man passes from the threat of Paradise Lost to the promise of Paradise Regained, open the Bible in the middle and read about another garden—the Garden of Gethsemane.

The Bible is not a straight line; it is a spiral, sometimes receding, but always moving forward again to a higher level. The movement is forward, not in circles. History to the Jews was the sphere in which God's purpose was unveiled and made known to man. The Old Testament finds its consummation in the New, and the New Testament finds its aspiration in the Old. As Augustine put it,

> In the Old Testament the New lies concealed.
> In the New Testament the Old is revealed.

When we say that the Bible deals with the basic themes of God, man, life, sin, death, and destiny, the emphasis is on the first word—*God*. The reason the Bible can interpret man's existence is God. Because it begins with the accepted fact of God, the Bible rests upon the faith that beyond all the mysteries, superficialities, and changes of the world and life in it, there is Someone by whom our life was created and is sustained.

It is true that the biblical representation of God is not always consistent. That makes the Bible all the more real and genuine, because the experiences and awareness of God were gradual and growing, more sensitive and acute in some people than in others. At the climax, in Jesus of Nazareth, the picture and meaning of God become clear.

Man's life on earth began well, but very quickly something happened that separated him from God. We call it "sin." If the first revelation the Bible makes about man is his sin, the second thing it shows is his discontent. Man realized that he was not meant to be separated from God. How is he to get back? Then the Bible gives us that great truth that there is more than merely a hunger after righteousness; it shows that there is a way for that hunger to be satisfied.

What a cruel hoax it would be to point out our sin to us—Paradise Lost; to show us our yearning search for something we feel is there for us, and then leave us in the confusion that sees no purpose, no meaning, no way out—hopeless futility. But the Bible shows us how Paradise may be regained—through faith in Jesus Christ. The experiences with God of men and women in the Bible are reproducible in us.

How would it be if a law was enacted which read

BE IT HEREBY RESOLVED
That every ten years all people shall forget whatever they have learned about the Bible, and begin the study all over again.[3]

This is what Bible scholars and translators are constantly doing, not every ten years, but every year, almost daily. And we need to do the same thing.

We say that the Bible is the textook of our faith. And it is. Textbooks are constantly revised, although they keep the same basics. There is always new knowledge to be considered. The new knowledge and experience is put alongside the old and evaluated and interpreted.

For the first twelve years of my Christian life I looked at the Bible as I was told, naively accepting all of it as of equal value. In high school I was introduced to some good Bible study, but it was strictly content, mostly literary content at

---

[3]Following Robert McAfee Brown, in *The Bible Speaks to You* (Philadelphia: Westminster Press, 1955) 87, whose very similar recommendation was, "Be it hereby enacted: that every three years all people shall forget whatever they have learned about Jesus, and begin the study all over again."

that. At Hardin-Simmons University, a Baptist school where Bible courses were required, again about all I was taught was content. I am grateful for that. It was at the Yale University Divinity School that I was introduced to a deep, reverent, historical, literary, and critical study of the Bible. This was done by devout men who were gifted scholars. More than that, they were committed Christians. They were at home in the ancient languages, archeology, science, and related fields. Under their tutelage, the Bible became for me "The Book That Is Alive."

When it comes to the matter of the inspiration of the Bible, I would like to say, "I Believe the Bible is the Word of God," and let it go at that. Or even, "I believe the Bible is the inspired Word of God," and let that be enough. But there are those who will not allow that. They insist that I spell out what I mean by such things as "inspiration," "Word of God," and they ask about "inerrancy." I don't mind doing that, but I do object when my spelling doesn't agree with their spelling, and they say that I can't spell.

This issue is not new. My own denomination has been plagued with it for more than two decades. So have others. In the middle 1800s Frederick W. Robertson, an Anglican preacher in Brighton, England, said that some Protestants of his day seemed to say,

> Here is the Bible; read it for yourself; but these doctrines, and no others, you must find in it; inquire freely, but at your peril arrive at any other conclusion than this.[4]

I cannot accept the theory of biblical inerrancy, not even that the "original autographs"—which no one has ever seen—were inerrant. (Perhaps those supposed originals

---

[4]Quoted by James R. Blackwood, *The Soul of Frederick W. Robertson* (New York: Harper & Bros., 1947) 45.

were lost to keep us from worshipping them instead of God.) Those who make such a claim for the Bible ridicule the Mormons for making the same claim for what was written on some golden tablets by an angel named Moroni— which no one, other than Joseph Smith, has seen. The inerrantists are well marinated in the juices of their own infallibility. I do not need their ideas of inerrancy to assure my belief in the Bible.

The "inerrancy" of the Bible is due to the accuracy of its portrayal of people as they were, and are. The people of the Bible are the same as people today; only the names and circumstances are different. Some Abraham still leaves an Ur of the Chaldees, not knowing where he is going or why, but compelled by the inner feeling of "a promise." David is as real now as then, for there is the same lust for power and women, cruelty mixed with deceit, combined with devotion to God and what is right, ending in a remorse and repentance which throws itself on God. There are Hoseas whose wives have been unfaithful, and Tamars who are the victims of incest and rape. Peter's vacillating personality lives on; so does Judas's treachery. The biblical people struggled with the same issues of life in the same emotional stress that we face. It is in that sense that the Bible is *inerrant*.

For fifty years my approach to the Bible has been one of reverence, belief, honesty, integrity, and commitment. All of this has added to my appreciation; none of it has distracted me from its basic purpose, nor clouded my belief. Of course there are parts of the Bible that cannot be proved, just as God cannot be proved. Those parts are experienced, just as God is experienced. Faith is believing in things that are not yet proved, that are out ahead.

It does not bother me that fallible men did not decide the completion of the Old Testament canon until ninety years after Jesus, or that there was confusion about the legitimate New Testament books for more than 300 years, or that other fallible men made mistakes in copying and allowed their own bias to creep into marginal notations and that later copyists included some of those comments in the text itself. (This same thing was done by a man named Scofield during the early part of this century, and is being done by others during the later part of this century.) I give thanks for the translators who have worked against great odds to give people the Word of God in their own language.

We live in the constantly increasing tensions and pressures of a crowded, busy time. The knowledge explosion baffles us. New issues repeatedly press in on us, demanding our attention, and calling for us to make decisions. What does an ancient collection of writings have to do with us in our kind of world? Why should we read or pay attention to the Bible? Some people idly let the question answer itself, assuming there is no reason to read it. And they are right, *if*:

> if the present can be understood and lived effectively without any perspective from the past;
>
> if there is no curiosity about the influences that have given our civilization its characteristic marks;
>
> if there is nothing uncomfortable in being ignorant of the inspiration that has created our greatest art, literature, music, ideas, and ideals;
>
> if the newspapers, magazines, and television can answer the ultimate questions we must ask;
>
> if we want to know nothing about God, man, life, sin, death, destiny, Jesus Christ and his ideals and ethics;
>
> if we do not want a way out of the mess we are in.

For me, there is a deep reverence for, a strong belief in, and a firm commitment to the Bible. I say with the song that children learn,

Holy Bible, Book Divine,
Precious treasure, thou art mine;
Mine to tell me whence I came;
Mine to teach me what I am.   —John Burton

✝ Looking at Jesus Christ
(Our Eternal Contemporary)

I could be a comfortable humanist, were it not for Jesus of Nazareth. Perhaps it would be easier if this Jesus would just go away. But he hasn't, and he won't; not ever, once we have met up with him. There is something disturbing about this Jesus of Nazareth.

What is it about Jesus that has caused people of varied cultures and times to say that he has been contemporary with every generation and will continue to be? What makes Jesus as relevant and meaningful to our time as he was for his own?

Jesus' importance does not come from the place where he grew up. He was no Socrates from Athens, no Caesar from Rome, no illustrious rabbi from Jerusalem. He was an itinerant from Nazareth. Nazareth was such an insignificant place that it is mentioned in the Bible only in reference to Jesus. Neither the Jewish Talmud nor the historian Josephus mentions Nazareth. In referring to Jesus, Nathanael asked, "Can anything good come out of Nazareth?"

(John 1:46). Jesus gave the town such distinction that he is called "Jesus of Nazareth." How? By who he was, what he said, and what he did.

Was it his moral-ethical teaching? Yes, in part, for those teachings are unsurpassed. Was it his idealism? Yes, for those ideals are yet to be attained. Was it his devotional-religious quality? Again, yes in part, for he showed the closest possible relationship with God. Was it his life? Yes, for his life was the noblest that history has seen. All these things, and more, are reasons for Jesus' continuing relevance.

However, the strongest basis for Jesus being our eternal contemporary is found in the New Testament:

> . . . you shall call his name Jesus, for he will save his people from their sins. . . . and his name shall be called Emmanuel (which means, God with us).
> —Matthew 1:21, 23
> . . . in Christ God was reconciling the world to himself.
> —2 Corinthians 5:19

Since Eden until now, sin has been a constant in human life, causing separation from God to whom we need to be reconciled. Jesus Christ meets the need and shows how we are to find the way back to God. How Jesus does this is called the "Atonement." There are many theories about the atonement that are just that—man's efforts at explanation—and none is adequate. Suffice it to say here that Jesus' death on the cross was for the forgiveness of sin and reconciliation with God.

We ended the chapter on God by saying that in Jesus, God gave us something of himself that touched us at our "near end." Jesus of Nazareth is the most of God that we know. I do not believe that Jesus is all there is to know of God, just as the water that washes an island is not all there is to the ocean. To say that would limit any further revelation God might choose to make. But I do say that Jesus is as much of God as we need to know . . . for now. There is no need for me to try to "prove" anything about Jesus. He is a man of history. What we are to believe about him is another matter. I confess to problems with much of the current emphasis on the worship of Jesus. I can't do that. I respect, even revere Jesus, but God only is to be worshipped.

Since I believe there is only one God, I have difficulty accepting Jesus as deity, but I can believe in his divinity. Dictionaries equate deity and divinity. Perhaps this is because our language is not quite precise enough. To me, this is more than a matter of semantics. Deity is reserved for God alone. Divinity pertains to or proceeds from deity, that is, it is Godlike. Some portion of this divinity (image of God) is in us all. In Jesus that divinity was developed to the fullest possibility.

The option we have about Jesus is to believe or not to believe. I believe. I even believe that he is Savior-Messiah. In fact I can stand with the early New England Unitarian, William E. Channing, who said that,

> Jesus was one mind, one soul, one being, as truly as we are, and equally distinct from the one God.[1]

The most confrontational question any of us faces is, "What do you think of Jesus Christ?"

My favorite illustration of Matthew 22:42 comes from Dr. John Kelmam who reported one of the shortest sermons ever preached:

> A chaplain, on a day of storm and heavy rain, had to

---

[1]*The Works of William E. Channing* (Boston: American Unitarian Association, 1896) 373.

conduct parade services with troops in the open. He knew his business, and his address was short: "No man but a fool would detain you on such a day. My text is, 'What think ye of Christ?' and my sermon is 'What think ye of Christ?' Dismiss."[2]

Decision about and commitment to Jesus Christ is the essence of the Christian faith. To believe that in him we find what God means to man, what man should mean to God, and what man means to man, is to make Jesus the central fact of life.

Being a believer in Jesus, or becoming a Christian, is not merely becoming "interested in religion." In more recent years we have used the word "religion" more than we have used the word Christianity. We have talked more about joining the church than we have about accepting Jesus as Saviour. Most of us know what we mean. Perhaps, for the most part, the two things may be equated. But there is a real danger that we shall eventually substitute a human religiousness that develops into a civil-cultural religion. Christianity is not merely "religion." It is a God-centered revelation that produces revolution in the lives of people.

Sometime ago a college-chapel address was given on the meaning of Christmas. The speaker, not wanting to offend anyone, talked about the joy of the Christmas season, the flow of generosity which the season releases, the home ties which the occasion strengthens, and the general spirit of good will which the season seems to inspire. But he did not mention the birth of Jesus. When questioned about his omission, he replied, "It is possible to have Christmas without referring to Christ."

That is true. Even in Japan much is made of Christmas

---

[2]As reported by Edgar DeWitt Jones, *The Royalty of the Pulpit* (New York: Harper & Bros., 1951) 91.

as a commercial venture, although Japan is not a "Christian" nation. A lady in a shopping center saw a manger scene and exclaimed, "Look at that! The church is trying to horn in on Christmas."

We just cannot talk about "Christmas values" unless we maintain reference to Jesus Christ, the events of his life, and the teachings from which these "values" spring, and without whom it would be impossible to maintain these "values."

Historic Christianity has regarded Jesus Christ as central. Whenever Christianity has been a potent force in the affairs of men, it has been due to a real discovery of the decisive nature of Jesus Christ.

In our day there is laid upon us the necessity of being confronted with this Jesus of Nazareth. We need to meet him in such a way that he will become the central issue for us as he was to those first-century Christians and has been to countless followers since then. In being confronted with him we hear and see the full story of God's purpose. To meet him is something unusual, for something unusual happens.

We see the impact he had upon such persons as Matthew, Mary Magdalen, the Samaritan woman, Peter, Nicodemus, Zacchaeus, the blind beggar, and the others. We hear those disciples tell about him out of lives dedicated to him as Saviour and Lord. They seem to be possessed of a secret that gave life purpose amd meaning. They are convinced that this Jesus came from the living God. They believe he is the center and meaning, not only of life, but of history. Those disciples were persuaded, decided, committed people.

From the beginning, Christianity has been confronted with two major problems about Jesus:

1. His humanity.
2. His divinity.

Stangely enough, more argument has centered around his humanity.

Some of the most severe theological arguments in church history have been about Jesus' humanity. As early as A.D. 120 Docetism touched off a heated controversy that nearly tore the church asunder. They said that Jesus only *seemed* to be born as flesh and blood and body. So the church fought the Docetists and drove them out. A heretic named Apollinarius convulsed the church about A.D. 374, not by doubting Jesus' divinity, but by denying that he had a human will. So in 381 at the Council of Constantinople the church cast out the Apollinarians.

It is only in more recent years, mostly within the past century, that the divinity of Jesus has been challenged. Even then, most of the controversy has been, not so much about his divinity as such, but about the Virgin Birth being necessary for his divinity. And again the church has been rent and some Christians have been cast out. The more conservative Christians claim two major reasons for Jesus' divinity (deity): the Virgin Birth and the miracles.

I began with an uncritical acceptance of both. Later the Virgin Birth was cast aside as being unnecessary and incredible, especially in the light of almost every primitive religion having some similar story of miraculous birth for its deity. Then I came back to believe that I must not limit God in any way. What biologists have done in reproducing life as high up the scale as the salamander and the rabbit without any sexual contact is amazing. If human scientists can do that, what could God do, if He so chose? This analogy has weaknesses. In parthenogenesis only females are born to females where there is no male sperm. Jesus was certainly masculine. What science will do in the future with cloning, genetics (that genie is already out of the bottle), and other research remains to be seen.

The phrase "Virgin Birth" has more than one interpretation. A "virgin" could mean a young girl, with no sexual inference, although virgin usually implies no sexual intercourse. It could also mean a first birth, that is, a birth by a woman who has never before had a baby. Perhaps this is rationalizing, and I could cop out by saying, "What do I believe about Jesus' Virgin Birth? Exactly what the Apostle Paul said. And what did he say? He never mentioned it." Nor did Jesus himself make such a belief a requirement for following him. In these late years I cannot believe in the virgin birth, and see no necessity for it.

When I accepted Jesus as my Saviour and became a Christian at age twelve, I didn't even know what a *virgin* was. How could I be expected to understand what "virgin birth" meant? If I was accepted as a Christian then, why make virgin birth a litmus test many years later? I suspect that the majority of Christians, whatever their persuasion of faith, have had a similar experience. I have never heard of anyone who was making a profession of Christian faith, even adults, who was asked, "Do you believe in the virgin birth of Jesus?"

Matthew and Luke, the only New Testament writers who say anything about a Virgin Birth, trace Jesus' genealogy through Joseph, not Mary. The strongest protagonists for the divinity of Jesus in the New Testament are John and Paul. Neither directly nor indirectly do they depend upon a miraculous birth for their claims of divinity. While John does relate miraculous events, he is also careful to point out that Jesus did not claim to be the Son of God merely because of some wonder-working power.

If we believe that Jesus is divine merely because he wrought miracles, then if our faith in the miraculous is ever shaken, our faith in Jesus will go because the basis of our faith is gone. If the evidence for the credibility of miracles is weakened, then the mystic glory fades away.

What this implies is, if miracles are the best proof of

Jesus' divine mission on earth, then God can only be recognized in the miraculous. We need a deeper basis of faith, a more secure foundation than that. What if modern science is able to reproduce human life? What would that do to our faith? So far as I'm concerned, nothing. It would lessen my belief in God and my faith in Jesus *not a whit*.

Something came over those first people who knew Jesus that gave them a strange sense of his authority over their lives. But his authority did not mean regimentation. He did not make James like John, or John like Paul, or Paul like Peter. Each was different. Under Jesus' influence qualities and powers began coming out in those men unguessed before, qualities and powers original, individual, and creative. The more each became more truly himself, the more he became Christlike.

As this kind of experience, which no one can adequately put into words, progressed, the disciples moved up from one stage to another in their thoughts of Jesus. Harry Emerson Fosdick put it this way:

> At first they may have said, God sent him. After awhile that sounded too cold, as though God were a bow and Jesus the arrow. That would not do. God did more than send him. So I suspect they went on to say, God is with him. That went deeper. Yet, as their experience with him progressed, it was not adequate. God was more than with him. So at last we catch the reverent accents of a new conviction, God came in him. . . . God came into human life! they cried; God has come into human life! Divinity and humanity are not so separate that the visitations of the Eternal are impossible. "God is love; and he that abideth in love abideth in God, and God abideth in him"; Know ye not that ye are a temple of God, and that the Spirit of God dwelleth in you?" "In the beginning was Mind and the Mind was with God, and the Mind was God. . . . And the Mind became flesh, and dwelt among us (and we beheld his glory, glory as of the

only begotten from the Father), full of grace and truth."
So they sang it. God can come into human life because
God has come into human life.[3]

What did Jesus do to move into people's hearts and
lives so transformingly? What caused such decision, devotion, and commitment?

The first thing Jesus did was to call for change (Mark
1:15). No person can stand face to face with Jesus and feel
that he stands on equal footing. To honestly stand in the
presence of Jesus is to be confronted with ourselves as we
are. To meet him thus is to stand at the fork of life's road
and make a decision: to remain as we are and be done with
him, or to desire all that he has to offer so that we will be
done with all in our life that offends God.

Joanne Greenberg, who wrote "I Never Promised You
a Rose Garden," has a collection of short stories entitled
High Crimes and Misdemeanors. One of the stories, "Flight
Patterns," is a kind of retelling of the story of Jacob wrestling with an angel. In an interview, Ms. Greenberg said the
story had special meaning for her "Because we wrestle with
devils, but we wrestle with angels, too. . . . We talk a lot
about wrestling with our devils—our addiction, our evil. But
we wrestle with our good surely as much. It's a more heroic
story. It's a hardedged victory." Who *is* Jacob's adversary
in the Genesis account? Greenberg says,

> The Lord. And he allows Jacob to win. It reminds me of
> the Eden story. I don't think God kicked us out. We left;

---

[3]Fosdick, in his sermon "What Does the Divinity of
Jesus Mean?" in *Living under Tension: Sermons on Christianity Today,* 150-60 (New York: Harper & Bros., 1941) 156-57;
reprinted in *Riverside Sermons,* 265-74 (New York: Harper &
Bros., 1958) 270-71.

we outgrew Paradise. Adam's job was to name the crea-
tures. God gave us that knowledge. But now the job is
to name the stuff that's inside us, and that's harder.[4]

We are created in the image of God, and with the power
of self-direction we have so enslaved ourselves in our self-
chosen way of life that we are hopelessly caught. The only
solution is radical and total, reaching the original springs of
our life. We must become new creations through the re-cre-
ative power of Jesus Christ.

It is significant that belief in Jesus Christ supplies the
reactive (salvation) source which enables us to name and
face the stuff that's inside us. But it is never forced upon us.
We were created with self-consciousness and self-assertion
(free will). Both of these have caused us trouble. The problem is to bring about our re-creation and yet preserve our
self-respect and self-confidence. So God steps in through
Jesus. But we are on our own. We decide for ourselves. Even
not to decide is to decide. And we are responsible for any
decision we make.

The term "born-again Christian" came into prominence about a decade ago. Evangelical Christians, especially in the South, were so familiar with the term they
hardly blinked. Now "born-again Christian" has become a
glib code word for a particular kind of Chistian experience.
It is valid, but not the only way.

The phrase comes from John 3:3. A learned man named
Nicodemus had a conference with Jesus. We don't know
what was said during the course of that conversation. In all
probability, Nicodemus asked how he could participate in
this new kingdom of God Jesus was talking about. Jesus
answered,

---

[4]*The Christian Century* 102/36 (20 November 1985): 1064.

. . . unless one is born anew [again], he cannot see [enter] the kindgom of God.

An elaborate theology has been made of that sentence. From it comes the "born-again" concept of salvation.

In other places the New Testament gives a different answer. In Luke 10:23-37 (the Parable of the Good Samaritan), a man asked Jesus the same question Nicodemus had asked. He was told to be a good neighbor. But we hear nothing about a "be-a-good-neighbor" method of salvation.

In Matthew 19:16-22 another man asked how he could have eternal life in the kingdom of God. He was told to sell everything he had and give it to the poor. These days we are not told that "sell all you have and give it away" is the process of re-creation.

In John 8:1-11 a woman was forgiven who didn't even ask to be forgiven.

C. S. Lewis describes his coming to faith in quite another way. For this Oxford University professor it was gradual. Over a period of time, drawn by the reasoning of his mind, he took the intellectual route and thought his way to a decision about Jesus Christ.[5]

Another person described his turning point this way:

I simply made a declaration to Jesus Christ that I was going to relinquish as much of myself as I could to as much of him as I knew. There was no lightning bolt for me. But I came to a peace, a feeling that if I make it, fine, and if I don't, that's okay, too.

Jesus never gave a patent-medicine formula; he al-

---

[5]C. S. Lewis, in *Mere Christianity*, rev. and enl. ed. (New York: Macmillan, 1952).

ways gave a personal prescription that suited a specific need. There is no one way of decision that is more valid than another.

In one of the episodes of the TV show "Star Trek," the *Enterprise* and her crew come to a planet that combines first-century Rome and twentieth-century America in its culture. Caesar's proconsul presses Kirk, McCoy, and Dr. Spock into service as gladiators. After the usual number of close calls, the officers of the *Enterprise* are saved, at the cost of his life, by a huge gentle gladiator named Flavius, who preaches universal brotherhood and seems to worship the sun. When they are beamed back to their starship, the three officers muse over Flavius, puzzled by his worship of the sun. Uhoura, the communications officer, tells them that they have misunderstood Flavius: it is not the "sun" that he worships but the "Son."

"Interesting, even fascinating," says Spock. "Christ and Caesar—they have them both here as Earth did."

"And Christ is triumphing over Caesar—just as he did on Earth," murmurs Kirk. "It's happening once more. Wouldn't it be marvelous to watch it again?"

We *are* watching it again. Every Christian, even the non-Christian, ought to stop short. Perhaps there is life on other planets. Perhaps there is also an "Incarnation." The science-fiction writers think so. So do I. And I believe a "Jesus Christ" is there also. The important point is not whether this is true or not, but that Jesus *was* here on earth. And what are we to do about that? Do we wish to follow him or not? What are we going to do about him?

When Jesus was here he proclaimed the Good News of the acceptable year of the Lord. He asked people to make a personal decision about him and for them to commit themselves and follow him. When the disciples preached, they first stated the factual message of Jesus. They substantiated that by appealing to the Old Testament. Then they told of their own experience and related what had happened to others. Finally, they asked their hearers to make their own decision and declare their belief in Jesus and his message. That same method is still in use.

Yes, I could be a comfortable pagan, perhaps even a devout Jew, were it not for this Jesus. I don't think I could embrace any of the other world religions. Christian faith makes more sense than the alternatives. Jesus is so central a fact of life, so essential to Christian faith, that one must come to terms with him.

What think *you* of Christ?

✝ The Second Most Beautiful Words

If the most beautiful words in the English language are "I love you," then I submit that high on the list for the number two spot is "I forgive you."

Everyone of us needs to hear both statements. Deny us either and we are bereft. If we feel unloved, we are miserable. If we feel unforgiven, we are desolate. Not only do we need to hear these words and believe them, *we need to say them as well.* Both hearing and saying are important for our personal well-being and our spiritual health. A silly statement from Eric Segal's book and movie *Love Story,* "Love is never having to say you're sorry," brought out a lot of sentimentality a couple of decades ago. Of course love, when it causes hurt, says it's sorry—often! It is easier to believe that God loves us and forgives us than it is to forgive ourselves. And many times it is difficult for some to believe and accept God's love and forgiveness.

In my youth I heard a lot about "the unpardonable sin." That is, "Therefore I tell you, every sin and blasphemy will be forgiven men, but the blasphemy against the Spirit will not be forgiven" (Matthew 12:31; cf. Mark 3:29; Luke 12:10 for variations). Although the statement is attributed to Jesus, it is bothersome. It goes against the biblical concept that forgiveness is God's favorite word, His secret weapon to overcome man's rebellion. Forgiveness and reconciliation may well be one of life's grandest experiences; only love and acceptance may be stronger, and love is involved in both forgiveness and acceptance. Forgiveness is powerful for both the one who is hurt and the one who causes the hurt.

I've seen only two people who were convinced they had committed the unpardonable sin. The first was a patient to whom I was assigned in a class in the Psychiatry Department at the Yale University Medical School. The other was as pastor of a woman who tried multiple confessions of faith and repeated baptisms, but could not accept God's forgiving love *or forgive herself.*

Forgiveness is a two-way street. If offered, it may be accepted or rejected. If we will not accept, there is no way it can be forced upon us, not even by God. If rejected, what then? Offer it again, "seventy times seven," as Jesus suggested. If still rebuffed, then it's time to say, "I've done all I can. It's time to get on with life."

Self-forgiveness is difficult. Why such a morbid obsession with guilt? Perhaps it is because we feel we are so bad that not even God can forgive us. But even Paul, who called himself "the chief of sinners" (1 Timothy 1:15), knew God's forgiveness. Sometimes there is a desire for self-punishment. If we flagellate ourselves long enough we will experience it. Maybe it is pride that will not let go—too stubborn either to ask or to receive. Or, we got ourselves in, we will pay our own way and get ourselves out. In each case we are wanting to play God.

During almost a half century of preaching I have said

that the amazing thing about Christian faith is that it declares that God always gives us a second chance, often more. And I believe that. But recently something I had overlooked pricked me: God did not give Adam and Eve a second chance! One sin, and they were expelled from Eden. Neither was King Saul given a second chance when he didn't follow Samuel's orders (cf. 1 Samuel 15:24-26). I've often puzzled over this. The best I can say is that the writer of Genesis was giving an account of how separation from God began, and that disobedience of God is serious business. The King Saul episode doesn't make much sense. Samuel's "to obey is better than sacrifice" (1 Samuel 15:22) may be true, but it needs to be seen in a broader context. My sympathies lie with King Saul. He was a magnanimous victor who showed compassion for human life, until he tried to placate an angry Samuel who portrayed an angry God, and then Saul hacked King Agag to pieces. This is not a pretty picture of man . . . or God. In the later light of Jesus' teaching and example we get a better picture of God.

Human life is not one piece of cloth. It is an individual tapestry, with many colorful threads. The teaching of forgiveness is a thread moving through the Bible and forming the mosaic of a lovely piece of tapestry that keeps life developing and worth preserving. We speak of it often. We speak of it glibly. We offer it freely. Theology teaches us that unforgiven sin keeps us from fellowship with God. We are taught by psychiatry that a major reason for functional disorders and emotional upheavals is a sense of unforgiven guilt.

Perhaps the most significant time of worship in Judaism is the Day of Atonement, Yom Kippur. At the opening service, immediately after the organ prelude, the rabbi approaches the open Ark, the congregation standing, and says,

Father of mercies, in awe and deep humility, I stand before Thee on this Atonement Eve. In the midst of Thy people who look to me to lead them I approach the holy Ark. I have erred and sinned. Forgive me, I pray Thee. May my people not be put to shame because of me nor I because of them. . . . Heavenly Father, let me hear Thy voice saying, Be strong and of good courage. Give me strength, give me understanding, give me faith, for Thou alone are my hope, O God, my Rock and my Redeemer.

The service concludes a day later:

Reader: And now, at the close of this day's service, we implore Thee, O Lord our God: Let the year upon which we have entered be for us, for Israel, and for all mankind: A year of blessing and prosperity. A year of salvation and comfort. . . . A year of pardon and favor.[1]

The major reason for the existence of the Church as an institution is the declaration, "God was in Christ reconciling the world unto himself" (2 Corinthians 5:19). The major emphasis of the Christian Gospel is the message of God's forgiving love. Unless at some place in a service of worship forgiveness is both stated and offered, the point has been missed.

In Christianity it is not a person's past that is important. Rather, it is the person's future, based on repentance of past sin and the seeking of God's forgiveness that matters. Were it not for this fact of forgiveness, Christianity would not be known as "the religion of the second chance."

To get us deeper into some thinking about forgiveness, listen to this sentence from one of my professors, the

---

[1]*The Union Prayerbook for Jewish Worship*, part 2, newly rev. ed. (New York: The Central Conference of American Rabbis, 1958) 126 and 292.

late D. C. MacIntosh, Professor of Theology at Yale:

> No sin is unpardonable, once it is repented of; and yet all sin, so long as it is not turned away from, is unforgiveable.[2]

For one thing forgiveness of sin (or any wrong) is difficult. So often, forgiveness is presented as an easy thing, as though "Come everyone, have your sins forgiven," is something simple. Not so! It is hard to forgive sin. Hard for us. Hard for Jesus. Hard for God. "Which is easier," Jesus asked, during the episode of the palsied man, "to say, 'Your sins are forgiven,' or to say, 'Rise and walk'?" (Matthew 9:5)

Do you see what Jesus was implying? It is easier to tell a paralyzed man to walk, to meet any human need, than it is to say, "Your sins are forgiven."

When sin is taken seriously, when there is a sincere love for people, it is hard to forgive sin. When people are loved and when we see what sin actually does to people in the wrecking of their lives, the pain it inflicts on others, even on the innocent, we find it difficult to forgive that which causes such distress, hurt, trouble, and wreckage.

It is significant that Christianity has always associated and equated the forgiveness of sin with the cross of Christ. When we see Christ on the cross, we see the truth that to forgive sin is a hard thing to do. When the Christian gospel invites us to accept forgiveness, it does not try to attract us to a sentimental place where sin is condoned. It points us to the cross of Christ. And we can hear that cross saying that it is hard even for God to forgive. There is a solemn fact with which we are confronted: no one's sin is done with until it faces up to this process of God's forgiveness.

---

[2]Douglas C. MacIntosh, *Theology as an Empirical Science* (New York: Macmillan, 1919) 168.

It is commonly believed that the first word of Jesus from the cross, "Father, forgive them." was uttered at the time of the actual process of crucifixion. At the moment of the most excruciating pain, he prayed for those who were inflicting the pain. At that moment Jesus was the object of the most heartless cruelty man could inflict, and he prayed for their forgiveness. The suffering of the body and the anguish of the spirit must have been terrible. Yet, he forgot himself to remember the guilt of those who were so shamefully wronging him. Instead of burning resentment boiling itself over into an outflow of revenge, Jesus sincerely prayed that God would forgive them their sin.

We should not be surprised. After all, this is exactly what Jesus had been preaching. We would be astonished had he *not* done so, because it would mean those words of an earlier occasion had been forgotten:

> You have heard that it was said, "You shall love your neighbor and hate your enemy." But I say to you, Love your enemies and pray for those who persecute you, so that you may be sons of your Father who is in heaven; . . . "   —Matthew 5:41-45

So Jesus forgave. He practiced what he preached. And the demonstration of his own forgiveness is far more powerful than all his preaching. But the demonstration also reveals that the forgiveness of sin is a hard matter.

Look next at the conditions of forgiving sin. And note the plural use of the word *conditions*.

Most of us seem to think there is but one condition of forgiveness—*repentance*—and repeatedly we emphasize this. Repentance *is* necessary. There can be no forgiveness on God's part unless there is repentance on our part. Yet it is startling to note that the thing most often mentioned by Jesus as necessary for being forgiven is our own willingness to forgive those who have done us wrong.

This is a staggering thought. But a bit of reflection shows it to be true, and in another way points up the difficulty of forgiving. Forgiveness must begin at home; with God, and with us. So the condition of forgiveness is not just repentance only, except in the sense that the recognition of sin and the desire to be forgiven involves a turning to God which is necessary to be turned from sin.

Concerning the New Testament teaching of forgiveness, three things are clear. First, that God will forgive sin, whatever we have done, and the forgiveness is complete. Such forgiveness does not mean the erasing of a penalty, as we shall see later. It means the restoration of a broken relationship. The miracle of forgiveness is amazing: that God will take me back, although I have done Him wrong, and the relationship with Him shall be fully restored. That is incredible, almost too good to be true.

The second teaching is equally clear: that forgiveness is conditioned by and depends upon whether we are willing to be forgiving, and loving toward those who have wronged us.

No one finds it easy to forgive, for forgiveness is not our human way. We are more like Samson, eyeless in Gaza, praying about his enemies, not for their forgiveness, but for their destruction. Listen to him: "O LORD God, . . . strengthen me . . . that I may be avenged" (Judges 16:28).

Down history's corridors this spirit of revenge has burned itself into our heritage with its "eye for an eye" and its blood feuds where whole groups are punished for the misdeeds of one. If we are honest, we will confess that we are afflicted with such an attitude. Listen to Jesus:

> For if you forgive men their trespasses, your heavenly Father also will forgive you; but if you do not forgive men their trespasses, neither will your Father forgive your trespasses. —Matthew 6:14

And in the prayer he taught his disciples:

> And forgive us our debts, as we also have forgiven our
> debtors.   —Matthew 6:12

Or as Paul said:

> . . . and be kind to one another, tenderhearted, forgiv-
> ing one another, as God in Christ forgave you.
>   —Ephesians 4:32

A third consideration is that even forgiveness of sin
cannot remove the consequences. For example, I have had
a broken arm. Medically, it has healed. It has been restored
to its place of usefulness. Only an X ray can reveal that there
has ever been anything wrong. But the fact remains that at
one time that arm was broken.

Forgiveness is the restoration of a broken relationship,
not the remission of the consequences. It is not literally true
that to forgive sin is to make us as if we had never sinned.
That is not true in the consciousness of the sinner, nor is it
true in the consequences others may suffer. Forgiveness
means that sin is removed as the barrier that shuts off fellowship with God and our fellow man.

A body that is diseased because of sin is not restored
to health when the sin is forgiven. If one wastes the strength
of one's body in dissipated living, God will forgive the sin,
but the physical conditions can never be the same. The loss
of lives and the resultant sorrow caused by a drunken driver
can never be removed, although the sin may be forgiven.

It is disturbing when a woman confides to her pastor
the sin of infidelity, saying, "I'm not worried about God.
He forgives people like me. But what will my friends say?"

She has reason to feel that way, for friends are less
likely to forgive than God; not true friends, just acquaintances. However, if hers is remorse, not repentance; sor-

row for getting caught, and not fear before God, then she is misunderstanding forgiveness.

God forgave David for the sin of adultery with Bathsheba, and for the murder of her husband Uriah. But David did not escape the consequences of his sin. Many a bitter tear was shed by David over those consequences. But David did know the fact of God's forgiveness. And the people forgave him, too.

While it is true that we are not delivered from the consequences of our sin, it is likewise true that when we are forgiven we are put into a relationship with God that gives us a personal insight into the character of God which otherwise we could never know. If a person does not believe in God, he need not believe in the forgiveness of sin. On the other hand, the experience of forgiveness gives us such an assurance of a personal relationship with God that we cannot lose that consciousness of God without losing the sense of forgiveness.

Consider, finally, that first word of Christ from the Cross: "Father, forgive them; for they know not what they do" (Luke 23:34).

One New Testament word for sin means "to miss the mark." We can give the crucifiers credit for acting plausibly in what they thought were the best interests of the people and their religious life. They acted conscientiously according to their convictions. They were sincere in the belief that they were right. But even in being conscientious in their convictions of being right, they were wrong. They missed the mark.

When we sin we do not stop to figure out all of the consequences, nor the final results of our actions. Nor did the crucifiers. The crucifiers thought the responsibility was not theirs, for they were carrying out orders.

"Whoever is responsible for any errors in judgment in

this affair, it is not we," they said.

"Pilate is Governor, not I," said Caiphas.

"But it was you, Caiphas, who handed him over to me," replied Pilate.

"Yes, but the priests brought him in from a riot. Of course, we did have to send for him, and they found him hiding in a garden in the middle of the night. But his own disciple, Judas, told us where to find him," said the captain of the temple guard.

And so on and so on. Rationalizations, alibis, deft shunting of responsibility. The world is full of it *still*. Who started the war? The strike? The friction between neighbors? The family feud?

"I? *Never!* Not I! It was someone else. My record is clear. No one could have done more than I to keep the peace, to live up to the letter of the law. If only other people would do as well as I have done, there would be no cause for complaints."

At one place in the Apocrypha, the seer complains,

O Adam, what have you done? —2 Esdras 7:48[118]

Not *I*, but Adam![3]

Jesus—on the cross—was not literally saying that they did not know what they were doing. They knew, but they rationalized their actions. Judas was aware of his bargain. He said so. Pilate washed his hands with the realization that his decision was wrong. They did not act in ignorance. But

---

[3]Some of the foregoing is indebted to Frederick C. Grant, *The Passion of the King* (New York: Macmillan, 1955) 31-32

they did not comprehend how great their sin was. Nor do we. It is as if Jesus were saying, "Father, forgive them, for they need forgiveness so desperately."

And this is true of all of us. We do not know the full harvest that may result from what we do.

> Some cocktails at a party, not wrong in themselves, may result in a car wreck that causes death and brings sorrow into a home that is entirely innocent.
>
> A carelessly spread rumor, a nasty bit of gossip, or a significant silence may destroy a person's reputation.
>
> We may suppose our "tell it like it is" attitude causes but a momentary irritation. Yet we do not know how often we cause a depth of disappointment or distress which takes months, years, or a lifetime to heal.

As Jesus prays for their forgiveness, he knows he is being crucified for a cause worth the whole of life. He knows how foolish they are who think they can end his work by ending his life. He knows there are some things that nails cannot fasten to a cross. His teaching of forgiveness is one such thing. Now it is a force let loose in the world, backed up by that cross.

> The act of God that reconciled man was not a spoken word, but the Word made flesh.[4]

To see Jesus on the Cross is to see the high cost of forgiveness. It matters not what theory of the atonement we may hold, if any, or none. No theory of the atonement is ever satisfactory. There is this truth, though: all the explanations of the atonement—the cross—show that it was not easy for God or Jesus to forgive sin. It cost. And no one's

---

[4]George Docherty, *One Way of Living,* 108

sin is done with until the fact of the Cross is faced. It remains for us to receive this forgiveness.[5]

I believe in the forgiveness of sin. I've experienced it from God and people, more than once. I've even been forgiving at times, not often enough, but sometimes. I've even forgiven myself on occasion, and that's the hardest of all.

---

[5]I am indebted to Harry Emerson Fosdick for ideas regarding the difficulty and conditions of forgiveness: see his sermon "Forgiveness of Sin," in *Riverside Sermons*, 292-300 (New York: Harper & Bros., 1958). Fosdick warned that "When . . . you hear any one talking about forgiveness lightheartedly as an easy matter, you may be sure of this: he is not forgiving sin; he is condoning it, and that is another affair altogether." (294)

✝ The Necessity of a Sense of Humor

Humor is one of the best solvents in the world for the grit of irritation that gets into the cogs of life these days, and the man who can laugh at himself as well as at others will be among the last casualties in the war of nerves.
—Leslie Weatherhead[1]

The world is indebted to those who can create laughter, for we need all of it we can get. There is something about laughter that sweeps away annoyance, fear, worry, jealousy, and other emotional tensions.

Too many people have a tendency to take themselves too seriously. I have difficulty believing in, being serious about, or trusting anyone, or any group, that can't laugh at themselves. A sense of humor and the ability to laugh a

---

[1]*This Is the Victory* (New York/Nashville: Abingdon-Cokesbury Press, 1941) 164.

thing off have saved many an awkward situation.

Among my pet peeves is the way most artists have portrayed Jesus. Not only is Jesus usually pictured as effeminate, but always intensely serious and totally humorless. There is not even a twinkle in his eyes. Now, one can be serious *and* have a sense of humor. I believe Jesus was this way. True, he was a man of sorrows and acquainted with grief. But he also enjoyed life and had a choice sense of humor.

If humor has a rightful place in life, then it belongs in such serious times as illness and death. When one can smile at such a time it says much about the confidence one has about life. In more recent years humor and laughter have been seen as a distinct aid in dealing with illness. Two of our better writers, Norman Cousins and Joseph Heller, both of whom were stricken with debilitating disease, have written of the benefits of laughter in their recovery. No, laughter may not effect a cure, but it does assist in helping to cope.

Humor even has a place in a funeral service, not jokes, for that is inappropriate, and humor only when it depicts the person. Mary Ben Madden was a quietly humorous feminist. Cancer took her life. For her funeral I pictured a routine gala event that was receiving a new immigrant to heaven. Gabriel was there with a trumpet fanfare, Jesus and St. Paul were making welcoming speeches. Jesus told a few stories. Then St. Paul abruptly took over with some abstractions about "this mortal must put on the immortal." He talked on about miserable sinners, that no one was worthy of being in heaven, how suffering was so much a part of life, and began to say something about some of his best friends being women.

This new immigrant couldn't take it any longer so she spoke up in her nasal North Louisiana twang. And what was routine became something outrageously spontaneous.

"Now, Paul," she said—no *sainting* of him!—"now, just you wait. . . . When we have some time, and from what I hear we shall have lots of time, there are some things I want to say to you about some of your best friends being women. Oh, I know about Lydia, and the others. But I don't think you left us women much to go on. In fact, you did a lot of harm to the women of my day. Maybe some of us misunderstood what you wrote. That's easy enough to do, especially some preachers I know who are so insecure that they feel themselves threatened by women and are afraid they will take over the church. Well, if we women hadn't done some things we did, the church would be in worse shape than it is. But I'll talk with you later about that."

There is no one phrase or definition or even a single concept that can comprehend all the things that make us laugh. We may just smile to ourselves, or we may laugh out loud. We may run the gamut from a mere chuckle to an uproarious guffaw, a "belly laugh." We laugh in appreciation. We laugh in scorn. We laugh in love as we follow the faltering steps of a child just learning to walk. We laugh in harsh hatred as we follow the frantic stumblings of a trapped enemy. We laugh in acceptance of our fellow man. We laugh when our fellow man is rejected from group fellowship. We reveal much of our character by what make us laugh. Yet no one can define humor, not even the best humorist or comedian.

Note how the old master William Shakespeare used humor. When his audience was on the edge of their seats, tensed with the drama at some moment of climax, the audience was relaxed with some touch of humor, such as that of Mercutio in *Romeo and Juliet,* or the gravediggers in *Hamlet,* or good old gusty Falstaff.

We speak of crying one minute and laughing the next. Each is a basic emotion and closely akin. It makes sense for us to have a sense of humor in these days of hectic crises.

A sense of humor is a saving grace, relieving our tensions, getting our minds off ourselves, and helping us to live with what is.

If anyone is abnormally concerned with himself, the penalty is the lack of a sense of humor. Those who think more highly of themselves than they ought cannot stand off and look at themselves objectively and enjoy a good laugh at what they see. This is particularly true in the self-centered period of childhood. Children love laughter, but not when the laughter is directed at them. For them to be laughed at is to be ridiculed, and no child likes that. For that matter, neither does an adult.

A thing that bothers me about extremists of any kind is they can't laugh at themselves. Whether they be environmentalists, pro-choice or pro-life on the abortion issue, feminists, or whatever, they take themselves too seriously. There's no humor in them. I've learned that when I try to poke a "devil's advocate" jibe at them, they get upset. When Paul said "I bid everyone among you not to think of himself more highly than he ought to think" (Romans 12:3), I'd rather translate that to read *Don't take yourself too seriously.* There is no point that more aptly illustrates our failure to mature than the lack of a sense of humor.

No people in history have a deeeper sense of humor than the Jews. And no people have suffered as much adversity as they. The ability of Jews to laugh at themselves and their circumstances is a major saving grace that they have.[2]

Let's take a look at some biblical Jews, beginning with an unknown writer called Koheleth. The writer of Eccle-

---

[2]For a delightful look at Jewish humor, see *The Big Book of Jewish Humor,* ed. William Novak and Moshe Waldoks (New York: Harper & Row, 1981).

siastes saw life as it was—the iniquities of the human lot, the suffering of the just as if they had been wicked and the prosperity of the wicked as if they had been righteous. He became painfully distressed. In that distress he came to some conclusions:

> There is nothing better for a man than to eat and drink and enjoy himself as he does his work. And this, I find, is what God grants; for who can eat, who can enjoy himself apart from God.   —Ecclesiastes 2:24-25, Moffatt

> And I commend enjoyment, for man has no good thing under the sun but to eat and drink and enjoy himself, for this will go with him in his toil through the days of life which God gives him under the sun.
> —Ecclesiastes 8:15

In that way Koheleth says that it is better to enjoy the good things of life than to pine after the impossible. It is better to enjoy the fruits of one's toil, in spite of all that might happen, than it is to mourn for what is not. That is, do not grieve over what we do not have, but rejoice in what we do have.

Let's be careful, however, and not take this advice as a recommendation for a riotous, excessively greedy, hedonistic way of life. The ancient sage is saying that there is work to be done before enjoyment is won. He gives us an injunction to thankfully enjoy the good provided by God, for there is a God from whom life's blessings come freely as a gift to us all.

God in his providence saw fit to create us with a capacity for laughter. It is not irreverent to say that God Himself must have a sense of humor, else He would not have created monkeys, zebras, giraffes, kittens, puppies, or even babies, for that matter.

There is an abundance of delicate humor in the Bible, and some broad, rather crude examples as well. Both the Old and New Testaments have humor, although the New

Testament humor seems to stop with Jesus. It's difficult to find much humor in Paul. Perhaps there is more humor in the Old Testament because it is more people centered, while the New Testament is more about a message.

Biblical humor begins early in Genesis. A woman who is pushing ninety is told by an angel that she is pregnant. She and her century-old husband split their sides. Even the angel is bemused. He hides his face, but you can see his eyes twinkling at the incongruity of his announcement. The old woman, Sarah, and her husband, Abraham, were laughing at the idea of a baby being born in the geriatric ward with Medicare picking up the tab. One account says that Abraham laughed so loud that he fell on his face. The other account has Sarah hiding behind a door when she got the giggles. When God asked about Sarah's laughter, she was so scared that she denied the whole thing. Then God said, "No, but you did laugh" . . . smiling as He said it?

The best part of the story is that God wasn't upset with them for laughing. God told them that the baby was to be named Isaac, which in Hebrew means laughter. So God blessed their laughter and in a sense joined in it—God and man laughing together, sharing a glorious joke in which both are involved. (See Genesis 17:15-17; 18:9-15.)

There is Jotham's parable about the trees making their choice of a king (Judges 9:7-15). The olive tree, the fig tree, and the vine (the more acceptable members of the tree family) had various reasons why they could not serve, why they declined the honor. So the crown was reluctantly placed upon the worthless bramble. Does that parable have a suggested answer to the often-asked question, "Why don't we have better people seeking political office?"

Samson was a great practical joker. Look at him as he carries away the gates of an enemy city, much as a boy engages in a Halloween prank. See him tie two foxes together, set them afire, and turn them loose in the enemy's grain fields. Then listen to his riddle:

> Out of the eater came something to eat.
> Out of the strong came something sweet.
> —Judges 14:14

The riddle's answer was finally wheedled out of him by his Philistine wife who then gave it to her people. When they brought the answer to Samson, he paid off his wager and said,

> If you had not plowed with my heifer,
> you would not have found out my riddle.
> —Judges 14:18

Rather crude humor, to be sure, but it illustrates that to the writer humor had a place in the religious history of his people. And those stories must have regaled the campfire gatherings of men and boys when the oral historian told those tales to keep alive the traditions of the people. Can't you see the old fellows slapping their thighs and guffawing, "Boy, that ol' Samson was something else!" And the boys took him as their hero—until the next night when the stories were about Barak or Gideon or David.

Is there any more mocking irony than that of Elijah saying to the priests of Baal on Mount Carmel, "Cry louder!" when they already were shouting at the top of their lungs, and had been since morning? "Maybe your god is asleep, or off on a journey," Elijah continued (2 Kings 18:27). (The Hebrew infers that "maybe he's gone to the toilet," but the translators were more delicate.) Elijah was using satirical humor to impress the people with the reality of his God.

Certain conventions of Christianity have made both Christian faith and its founder gloomy. For them, the long-faced, sad-eyed Bassett Hound is a fitting symbol. Many of us have *Cruden's Complete Concordance of the Bible* on our bookshelves. In 1769 that same Cruden said, "To laugh is to be merry in a sinful manner." Too many Christians have adopted that attitude. Anything that is fun must therefore be bad, sinful.

To be a Christian does not mean to abandon amusement or fun or pleasure. Any amusement or pleasure by which we receive enjoyment to ourselves and do no harm to ourselves or to anyone else, we are perfectly free to use. We Christians have been so fearful of all merriment that we have let other forces take charge of it—the theater, art, and music. For too long we have been guilty of suppressing the fun life of the Christian. Indeed, such a nature as that of Jesus, so responsive, so subtle, so rich in imagination and in understanding of his fellow man would have been an anomaly had he felt only the tragedy and not the comedy of life.[3] But we need not theorize about Jesus. Look at the New Testament.

Jesus' first disciples were called in a bit of a jest. One day Jesus was walking along the Sea of Galilee, and he saw Peter and Andrew casting a net into the sea, for they were fishermen. He knew those men, and they knew him. Can't you see a bit of a smile around the corners of his mouth and a twinkle in his eye as he said, "Fellows, follow me and I'll make you fishers of men" (Matthew 4:19; Mark 1:17; Luke 5:10).

When Jesus spoke of the Pharisees as "sounding trumpets before them when they do alms," he was saying that when they took a basket of groceries to a needy family they

---

[3]For some insightful reading regarding life's tragic and comedic side (or life's tragedy and comedy), see Frederick Buechner's *Telling the Truth: The Gospel as Tragedy, Comedy, and Fairy Tale* (San Francisco: Harper & Row, 1977).

hired the Olympia Brass Band to accompany them and called in the TV cameras to record the "Live Aid" concert. A critic of Sir James Barrie, the playwright who gave us the whimsical *Peter Pan*, once said of him, "He rattled the cans when he brought around the milk of human kindness."

Jesus' exaggerations were a form of humor. The picture of an old busybody, with a stick of timber in his own eye, solicitous for the eyesight of a neighbor with a fleck of dust in his eye is ridiculous. Doubly so is the faultfinder hypocrite who strains out a gnat of unorthodoxy and then swallows a camel, humps and all, in personal practice. Such persons are like a pious seminary student who told his girlfriend that dancing was sinful. She squelched him by saying, "You don't dance, but you'll buy me a pizza and then try to squeeze it out of me before we get home."

Do you remember the story Jesus told about a man who had finally succeeded in getting the children to sleep when a neighbor came banging on the door asking for food for some unexpected guests who had shown up? The man got up and got the food. Why, he'd give the neighbor the whole house to keep him from waking the baby. What new father hasn't had the experience of walking and rocking a colicky baby to sleep in the wee hours? Even more ludicrous, what male of *that* day would be putting the children to bed? That was the wife's work.

Can we believe that no laughter was intended or did not occur when Jesus began telling the excuses of those men who wanted to get out of going to a dinner party they didn't want to attend? Come to think of it, are not many of the excuses we offer just as hilarious?

Jesus went to parties, especially wedding feasts. He was a welcome guest at such affairs. His enemies accused him of being a gluttonous winebibber. It is strange that some people think it impossible to have fun without getting drunk and/or making a fool of yourself. Many a hostess thinks nothing of it if a guest refuses a cup of coffee, but to refuse a cocktail? That is a personal insult!

No man could look at human nature as Jesus did without smiling. Humor is as old as speech. Laughter rings around the world. And Galilee had its mirth, too, and even we can hear it. True, Jesus was a man of sorrows and acquainted with grief. But he also enjoyed all life that the Father gave him. His mirth was consistent with a tender compassion for all that is frail and with profound reverence for all that is sublime in human life.

After all, who has more right to humor, fun, and the full enjoyment of life than the Christian? When the world around the person who has no belief in God comes to pieces there is nothing except despair. For the Christian, who knows that the real joys of life cannot perish, there is joy. The Bible calls it "joy unspeakable and full of glory." The Christian can experience suffering and pain, he can go through sorrow. Often the Christian's laughter may be silenced. But nothing can take away the smile of confidence.

Christian faith makes room for the hard facts of life. It never minimizes tragedy and sorrow. It takes into account sin and the suffering caused by it. But Christianity never despairs; it always holds out hope.

In Andrew Greeley's novel, *The Cardinal Virtues*,[4] a young priest assigned as associate to an older priest asked, "You know why Jesus went out into the wilderness by himself?"

"The Bible says to pray."

"Nah, to laugh. He found our seriousness and solemnity hilariously funny, and he didn't want to hurt our feelings by laughing in our faces."

When we can laugh it means the events around us have

---

[4](New York: Warner Books, Inc., 1990) 14.

not gotten us down. In the midst of the world's raucous turmoil a jubilant voice comes chiming through the centuries from a man standing on the shore of a Galilean sea. The tribulation of the world is in his heart, but the laughter of heaven is in his eyes and voice as he says, "Be of good cheer, I have overcome the world" (John 16:33).

✝ What about Miracles?

I've seen some miracles. Maybe not the kind usually thought of, and you may not agree with my classification of the miraculous. Some lines from a popular song will illustrate:

> Welcome to my world,
>   won't you step right in.
> Miracles still happen,
>   every now and then.

The sophisticated world in which we live is unresponsive to almost anything to which the term "miracle" is attached, especially if it is recorded in the Bible or has anything to do with religion. When the miracles of the Bible, either those of the Old or the New Testament, are considered, people generally come under two broad classifications: those who accept the accounts uncritically simply because they are recorded in the Bible; and those whose background, based on what they consider to be a scientific understanding of the modern world, makes them skeptical on general principle. However, most of us have discovered in our contacts with life that factors do enter in that cannot be explained by what we know of the ordinary processes of the natural world.

In our enlightenment we must remember that the people of the ancient world, with their limited and often naive view of nature, lived in what to us would be considered a fairyland. Anything that could not be explained by the ordinary course of events was neatly classified as a miracle. But are we too far advanced when we try to explain electricity or television or radar? Or when many among us still believe in "gris-gris dust," or the signs of the Zodiac or astrology or the occult?

While biblical writers, and even the church fathers, did not hesitate to record or believe in miracles, they were often more up-to-date than we give them credit for being. Augustine, who lived some 1,500 years ago, exhibits a quite modern viewpoint when he says that miracles are not contrary to nature; they are only contrary to nature so far as it is known by us (*The City of God* 21.8).

There are two strikingly contradictory positions of this age in which we live: on the one hand our credulity, and on the other hand our skepticism. We are quite willing to accept the most improbable in the realm of the physical, especially if it has the word "science" (or medicine) attached to it; whereas in the realm of faith (religion) we raise all sorts of questions about the simplest things.

Physical wonders have ceased to amaze us because we have seen so many things that once would have been characterized as miracles actually come to pass before our own eyes. In my own lifetime such things as radio, television, atomic energy, space exploration, and computers have been born, grown to maturity, and become commonplace.

Only thirty-five years ago I was one of two men in the

city of Ruston, Louisiana (the home of a fine technological university) who openly stated belief in the "miracle" that man would one day go to the moon. The other was a math professor whom everyone considered a crackpot, anyway. What did they think of me? I even believe in UFOs and life on other planets. Who are we to be so smugly superior as to think that only this small speck in the universe called Earth has intelligent life? If we believe in God, we can't limit God. And if anyone raises the question about "salvation" for other "beings." God can take care of that, too. Anyway, maybe those other beings didn't sin and mess things up as we have. From a college course in "Modern British and American Poetry" I remember a line from a British poet named James Stephens: "That star [earth] went always wrong, and from the start I was dissatisfied" ("What Thomas an Buile Said in a Pub").[1]

Since then I've held to the idea of life on other planets, quietly at first, but out of the closet since 1960.

I'm not a science-fiction buff, but have read it since the Buck Rogers and Flash Gordon comic strips. Who (other than Dick Tracy) would have believed a wrist-sized radio-TV a decade ago? The miracle of microchips made that possible. Modern genetics will produce miracles that are unbelievable. That genie is out of the bottle. And what about the mechanical heart? It is a reality. Now that it has been done, it is only a matter of time until it is refined and perfected. Bypass surgery and heart-valve replacement, less than twenty years old, are now commonplace procedures. I've had the bypass and am grateful that it came in my lifetime.

Such wonders have accustomed us to believe that

---

[1] *Modern British Poetry*, ed. Louis Untermeyer (New York: Harcourt, Brace, and Co., 1936) 338.

nothing is impossible in a technical-scientific world. We are not so advanced in the moral-spiritual world. There we remain skeptics.

Earlier generations of Christians, even fifty years ago, and still some today, were impressed with the apologetic value of miracles. That is, miracles were used to substantiate God, and prove Jesus as being the Son of God. I would say that miracles as evidence of God are unimportant; the concept of miracle is important.

I would not try to give a rationalization or explanation of biblical miracles. Some such explanations that I have read, both by skeptics and believers, are more incredible than the miracle itself. It is obvious that our understanding of natural law is so limited that we are rash to say that anything violates it. The more we are able to classify the laws of the natural world, the better we are able to understand what happens. It seems logical to me that there are also spiritual laws that are unknown to us, and if we were able to classify them we would be better able to understand spiritual things.

The fact that we may account for a miracle by a natural explanation in no way involves surrender of belief in the miraculous. If God enters the situation, the miracle is still there. In fact, the truest understanding of biblical miracles is at this point. It is not the event, but the fact of God in the event that is vital. The Genesis record says that when the Israelites crossed the Red Sea, God caused a strong east wind to blow to part the waters, thereby giving us the method used. The miracle does not consist in a wonder that is contrary to all experience or possibility, but that God entered the situation in a natural way. Even ancient rabbinical literature has this natural explanation.

More miraculous than "the parting of the waters" was the faith that caused those Israelites to start walking toward the other shore, with one Israelite already up to his nostrils in the water, crying, "Come on, you schlemiels, let's go!" not knowing if the waters would part or not. It is no argument against the divine origin of a thing to be able to explain it by natural causes. And the same thing is true of the healing miracles of Jesus being explained in psychosomatic terms.

We might as well recognize that there is no ultimate rationale that will explain or account for what we call a miracle. Compare almost any biblical miracle with the modern wonder of radar, which enables us to see through fog or night. One is scarcely more marvelous than the other. Though we know much about electronics, the ultimate nature of electrical energy that makes the modern miracle possible eludes our understanding. We use radar to bring airplanes to a safe landing, though we may not in the last analysis explain how it works. How, then, can we deny the miraculous grace of God that safely guides us through the fogs of life just because we can't explain how it works? We put our lives in the hands of pilots who depend upon radar. Why are we reluctant to put our lives in the hands of God?

For most of the healing miracles of Jesus we can give a good rationale in modern terms, especially in terms of psychosomatic or funtional disorders. In the Synoptic Gospels, Jesus rejected the role of "wonder worker." He carefully avoided the spectacular in his work. Yet the element of compassion in his ministry was strong. Jesus did perform what were called miracles. But the Gospels show him as more interested in opening *spiritually* blind eyes, unstopping *spiritually* deaf ears, and raising *spiritually* dead lives than in performing the physical acts attributed to him. And he was less successful in this. One also wonders if there were any healing *failures*? I suspect there were. If there were, they are not reported. I'd like to know the reactions if some were not physically healed.

Belief in the miraculous healing of bodily diseases has been with Christians since the time of Jesus. Such shrines as Lourdes in France and Saint Anne de Beaupre in Quebec have long histories. Medical science has examined many of the "reported cures" from these places and has no explanation for many of them. On the other hand, some have not been confirmed.

I grew up in a Pentecostal tradition that believed in faith healing long before Oral Roberts and others gained national prominence. Although I have shed those Pentecostal teachings, I have kept up with the movement through such people as Starr Dailey, Louise Eggleston, Oral Roberts, and Katherine Kuhlman. No doubt, there is more to faith healing than many of us are willing to admit. It has been strange to observe the resurgence of interest in divine, or faith healing, that has emerged in recent years. Such opposites from Pentecostalism as the Episcopalians and Roman Catholics have emerged as strong proponents. The "Charismatic Movement" has been born in our day, and some "miraculous healings" have been reported.

I would not deny the validity of those healings. In fact, I would say I believe in the possibility of the healing of diseases that baffle human care—not just functional disorders, from which a person can suffer intense pain, but also from organic disease. A talk with any physician will confirm that something sometimes happens that cannot be explained. I also believe in prayer for the ill. To pray for them means also to use the best skills of modern medicine. That's the New Testament "anointing with oil," I think. More often I pray that the sick person will feel the grace and presence of God to cope with the illness, for not everyone is healed, nor does everyone remain healed. What then?

From 1962 till 1973 my first wife suffered from two forms of invasive cancer. She was given the best of medical care, including some experimental treatments. Many prayers were offered in her behalf. A Roman Catholic monsignor made a novena (*nine days'* devotion, hoping to gain some special grace). One of her doctors was a Roman Catholic "charismatic." Jewish rabbis and congregations prayed, as did Moslems and Buddhists.

Many well-intentioned people would say to us, "If you have faith enough, and if it is God's will (note that!), healing will come."

My reply was something like this:

> "Now wait a minute! When you start talking about faith, especially someone else's faith, be sure you know what you're talking about. And when you assign healing, or lack of healing, to God's will, you are making God rather arbitrary, and you are causing the ones healed to feel smug and superior and the ones not healed to feel rejected by God, and even causing them to feel that God does not love or care enough for them. And this is not true!"

One dear soul said to my wife, "Tragedy does so color one's life, doesn't it?" To which she spunkily replied, "Yes, and I intend to choose the colors!"

I respect privacy, mine and yours. But we ask people to share their personal testimony of salvation because by doing so someone else may come to know Jesus Christ. Those who have been healed are asked to tell their experience in order to encourage another.

Why should we not ask those who have *not* been healed, but who have found an extra portion of the grace of God to live radiant lives, to share that as a way of encouraging others? To me, such radiant living is a far greater testimony of the miraculous power of God than even healing would be. Any healed person would rejoice. Why can't we see and accept gracious, courageous, joyful living, despite adversity, as witness to the miracle of God's grace?

There are those who are living great lives in spite of adversity; not all of them are Christian, or even believers in God. They have not been physically healed, but they exhibit in their lives the miraculous. They are radiantly alive. And the thing is, this same miraculous grace of God which makes for victorious living may be ours, too, if we want it, will take it, and choose the right colors.

✝ A Christian Quest through Faith, Doubt, and the Church

The Christian faith is a striving, not an arriving. One begins the Christian quest with whatever amount of faith one can muster; belief, to whatever extent, comes along the way. We cannot prove the Christian faith. There is an indirect verification of Christian faith because it makes more sense out of the facts of life than any of its alternatives.

Faith is the great word we use in church. *Doubt* is considered the enemy of faith. So we have exiled the word doubt from most ecclesiastical circles. We speak of it only in guarded whispers, and even then usually among trusted friends. In the churches I have pastored, I have encouraged a healthy respect for honest doubt. Doubt is a vital part of real faith. Reverent as we are, respectfully as we may listen, convinced though we may be, everyone of us must honestly say what that man said to Jesus, "I believe; help my unbelief!" (Mark 9:24).

Doubt (skepticism) is one of the noblest powers we have. Without that capacity there would be no progress, only docile, unquestioning acceptance of the status quo. Scientific advance begins with someone's skepticism. Someone had to doubt the idea that the earth was flat and the sun moved around it. Pioneers in any field emphasize faith. That is, while doubting some old concepts, they affirm their faith in new ideas and possibilities. For them, there is always something more. The dictionary I used in colledge (1935–1939) defined *atom* as "one of the hypothetical, indivisible parts of which all matter is supposed to be formed." See what has happened because some doubted the words "hypothetical, indivisible, and supposed to be."

Jesus himself was a great doubter. The Law said, "An eye for an eye and a tooth for a tooth." The Law said, "Hate your enemies." The Messiah was to make war on Rome and restore the Davidic kingdom. Popular belief said that the Samaritans were an inferior people who did not deserve to mingle with Jews in society, not even to worship with them. Jesus doubted all those things. And more.

There are those who say Christian faith may be inherited. No. One may inherit a creed, but not faith. Faith is personal. Faith is as much a verb as it is a noun. Jesus "faithed" his way to the cross. He may have *believed* the cross was the will of God for him, but it was *faith* that took him there. Faith comes from having struggled for it in one's own experiences. The manner makes no difference, so long as it is one's own.

The Bible is said to be a book of faith. It is also filled with the experiences of those who wrestled with their uncertainties. The trouble is that we know the faith of the great saints, but we hear little about their doubts.

The sturdiest faith of biblical characters and historical

Christian personalities has come out of their struggle with unbelief and doubt. Faith may never completely dispel all doubt. But the central experience of a believer is to honestly go through his disbelief until he begins to doubt his doubts.

Every religious person faces the temptation of hypocrisy. Religion organizes its fellowship into churches, its thought into creeds, and its standards into codes of conduct. Thus it becomes somewhat easy to assume these outward exhibitions and professions of religion. There are those whose lives do not demonstrate outwardly what they say they profess.

The problem we face is not just that kind of hypocrisy. Multitudes these days are making no profession of religion at all. They make no pretensions of faith.

Hypocrisy, like Janus, has two faces. Some people are hypocrites because they profess a Christian faith that they are not living. Others are hypocrites because deep within and in outward action they are practicing a Christian faith, drinking from a fountain they do not acknowledge. This latter is in such wide use that I want to challenge it. Consider these friends of ours who say they are not religiously hypocritical because they profess nothing religious. I won't consent to that. Many such friends of mine are practicing Christianity in almost everything except public profession of faith in Jesus Christ and church membership. We call them "good people outside the church." We often complain that it is difficult to distinguish between them and those who are in the church.

Most of us distrust pretension in religion. We are wary of wearing our religion on our sleeves. I am weary of people who say "Praise the Lord!' with the frequency of an athlete's "You know." When we try to reduce our professions of religion to a minimum we may think we are being honest. But honesty is a virtue too profound for that. Perhaps all of us need to square what we seem to be with what we are, on both sides of this matter. In a way that we may not have considered, this could mean for us to be as Christian as we are. It is interesting to note that Jesus bore down on this aspect.

We know how emphatically he attacked hypocrisy. Two things Jesus could not stand: cruelty and sham. We are familiar with what he said about sham, all the way from the mild—

> When you give alms, sound no trumpet before you, as the hypocrites do in the synagogues and in the streets, that they may be praised by men. . . .   —Matthew 6:2

to the harsher—

> Woe to you . . . hypocrites! for you are like white-washed tombs, which outwardly appear beautiful, but within they are full of dead men's bones and all un-cleanness. So you also outwardly appear righteous to men, but you are full of hypocrisy and inquity.
> —Matthew 23:27-28

So we say that is what hypocrisy meant to Jesus: trying to appear better than we are.

But there is another side. What about appearing *worse* than we are? Jesus had something to say about that, too:

> . . . Nor do men light a lamp and put it under a bushel, but on a stand, and it gives light to all in the house. Let your light so shine before men that they may see. . . .
> —Matthew 5:15-16

To have light and keep it in the dark, to have faith and keep it covered up, to have some radiance—though it be but the slender flicker of a candle—and hide it, to refuse to set it out where people who need it can get its full effect, that too is hypocrisy. That also is failure to square what we seem to be with what we are.

There is something to be said for people who succeed in showing their light rather than their darkness, their faith instead of ther fear, their best not their worst. I can be advocate and sing the praises of people who are better than they profess to be.

My best friend is not a professing Christian. He has nothing to do with the church. He is not antagonistic, just indifferent. Yet, from many hours of talk and some forty years of observation, I know another side of him, the inner person. I know that he takes vacation time (he is a pediatrician) to give medical attention to migrant workers' children, or to American Indian tribal children, or to Arab refugee camps. He never deducts these expenses from his income tax. At odd hours he calls me to pray for him as he treats a seriously ill child, and he is at his wit's end. Why? Because inside him is a faith in something, in Someone he is reluctant to confess. He feels God is the unutterable sigh in the human heart. The best in him gets let out in spite of himself.[1]

We are accustomed to talking about those sorry people who assume the cloak of high religious profession to hide their inner villainy. Because they are so contemptible and can so easily be described as appearing to be better than they are, we have come to shy away from appearing to be as good as we are.

I can understand why many are reluctant to make any profession of or indentification with Christian faith. We are living, neither for the first time nor the last time in history, through days of rapid change. So much new knowledge has

---

[1] In the summer of 1986, Dr. Bruce Everist joined the Trinity United Methodist Church in Ruston, Louisiana.

been poured into our minds and so many extraordinary things have happened that the channels of our religious thinking have been flooded. The consequent confusion is so bewildering and the task of phrasing faith in the old formulas so impossible that many think it insincere or unnecessary to make any profession involving religious faith. So we have, if not unbelief, at least indifference.

As a preacher, my aim has been to try to entice more Christian faith and character in a time which desperately needs it. Perhaps there is another aim which I have missed. What if we could get the Christian faith and character already existent and now under a bushel out in the open on a stand where it could give some light? What if the hidden unprofessed, reluctantly admitted, inoperative Christian faith could be set out where this age could feel its full effect? What if we could persuade some that, while of course it is hypocritical not to be as Christian as we seem, it is also hypocritical not to be as Christian as we are? What we do not express tends to die and what we do express tends to live. Keep a candle under a bushel long enough and for lack of oxygen it will go out. Of course a candle *burns out* when it is exposed.

As for being Christian, I dare say that many in this generation are not thinking their way out of Christianity but are talking themselves out of it, or by inertia taking themselves out. To be irreligious has become an "in" thing, a conventional thing as conformist as what they say they disdain in those who find Christian faith meaningful. The Christian faith and heritage have not been entirely without effect. There is within us a sensitive feeling about what Jesus stands for. But unless something is done in response to those feelings, that candle goes out.

Let your light shine! Some of us tried, and still try that. We took our stand on the best of life we could be, the noblest faith we believed, revealed in as much of Jesus Christ as we could comprehend. To that we committed our lives. Our candles flickered and burned low, for some of us had less to offer than others. But we tried to keep them burning, out where they were supposed to be.

We need light. Jesus came into a generation which needed light. Under his influence fell a small group of, for the most part, ordinary people who were persuaded by him to take such light as they had and put it on a candlestick. And they did, with revolutionary consequences. The world's darkness has never been able to quench that light. At least we can do as much for our generation. At least we can be as Christian as we are, however little or much.

Some forty years ago, a brilliant young friend asked me, "Why do you do it? Why do you preach Sunday after Sunday, sermon after sermon, knowing very well that only a very few will ever really notice or remember anything you say, much less let what you say change their lives? Why do you do it? What's your motivation?"

There is no terminus to belief or Christian faith. Both are ongoing, changing, and growing, sometimes even maturing. There are some conclusions one comes to, however, and some observations to make about the continuity.

One such observation is about the church. The church must have a divine quality about it, else it could not have survived almost twenty centuries of human weaknesses. In many ways the church is a failure, a magnificent failure. In more ways the church is a glorious success. One can point out such things as the Crusades and the centuries of bickering among Christian churches. Or one can stress such things as the church's building hospitals and schools where there were none.

There is no need to catalogue the failures of the church nor to make a list of its problems. The church has always had problems. Something would be wrong if it didn't. Almost every denomination of churches is engaged in internal conflict, usually revolving around some doctrinal dispute, and just as often the result of a power struggle. When some of us go to our national meetings we are made to feel like bastards at a family reunion. Individual churches have financial difficulties, attendance problems, and differences of opinion as to what constitutes the gospel. Why should anyone even want to join up with such a belabored institution? Or why ask anyone to join?

Many people have left the church. They say they are not "leaving Jesus," just leaving the church, because they see no need for it as an institution. They can be Christian without belonging to a church, they say. With that latter statement I would agree. Belonging to a church does not make one a Christian; faith in Jesus Christ does that. But I have observed that those "leavers" almost immediately begin organizing a structure which more than faintly resembles the church they have discarded—except the requirements for membership are more rigidly defined. This holds true at all levels of theological belief.

The liberals have their "underground church" movements.

The social activists have their strict conformity.

The conservatives have their businessmen's leagues and prayer-meeting, Bible-study, witness groups.

The ultra conservatives have their moral majorities.

All of them draw their followers from the Church, and then they have the temerity to ask the church for financial support.

Of course the church has its failures. The point is, the church *admits* its failures. The church *recruits* failures. Its sole requirement for membership is that the person applying admits his/her failures. Only the church takes us as we are in order to help us become what we ought to be. This is the true nature of the church. When we realize that, we will stop apologizing for the human failures and proclaim the divine feature: *The greatness of the Church is not in its membership, but its Lord.* Our need is not a restatement of what the church does or does not do, nor what it believes or does not believe. Our need is a reaffirmation that the church exists as the "Body of Christ." That is so searching a fact that soon or late we must come to grips with that and make a response to that. In "Bishop Blougram's Apology," Robert Browning asked,

> What think you of Christ, friend,
>   When all's done and said?
> It may be false, but will you wish it true?
>   Has it your vote to be so if it can be?

This is the arresting question we face every time we go into a church house, or even walk past. So, to answer the question the friend asked me years ago, "Why do you do it?" *Because I believe in the Church!*

The Church is not a "Book of Numbers" wherein sometime or other our name may have been written on its rolls. The church is the "Acts of the Apostles," volume 2 or volume 1992, where we go on with the story.

I grow weary of those who glibly say, "You don't have to belong to the church; just live by the Golden Rule and follow the Law of Love. The church isn't really necessary."

Bosh! Where did that Rule and that Law come from? If it were not for Him who founded the church no one would be bothered by that Rule. All this talk about a better world by letting a little love into your heart is downright silly unless we remember that the church is the soil in which the roots of that better world are nurtured so they can grow.

We can't escape that. We can laugh at the church, belittle it all we will, and criticize its members for hypocrisy. Then we must admit that the very ideals we say ought to be followed are alive today because the church has kept them alive. And those who stay out are trying to kill it off.

What we are confronting here is an ancient question, yet as modern as tomorrow. As a matter of fact, Paul asked it a long time ago: "Do you despise the church of God?" (1 Corinthians 11:22).

To be sure, plenty of people condemn the church as a camouflage for their own rejection of the life and character for which the church is standing. They blame the outward institution, whereas in fact they are not willing to accept the quality of faith and life for which the institution stands. They are like the man who complains about a volume of Shakespeare that the print is too small and the book is too heavy, when all the time he doesn't want to read Shakespeare at all, but the latest issue of *Sports Illustrated*. Many people blame the Church when really they just have no use for what the church represents.

It has been my privilege to see many parts of the world where the Christian faith is unknown, or at best only in a limited way, where Christian churches have never been, or where they stand in remote isolation. Against that background I have seen the finest of missionary lives, young and old, with a depth of faith the like of which I wish I had, with the best of education, possessed of unusual ability, and working against odds that seem insurmountable. Are they discouraged? Not at all. Although I'm sure the load gets mighty heavy at times. Are they weary in well-doing? Of course not. Although I'm sure they are very tired.

Each of those missionaries, each of those little meeting houses is speaking. One is forced to listen to what those meeting houses and our churches at their best are saying. Someone protests, "But listen how they stammer." Of course we stammer, some of us very badly. Yet, for all the stammering, consider what at best we are trying to say: "God was in Christ. . . . What do you think of Christ?"

Let the church die. Let generations rise that never knew the church. Let Jesus become a legend, the Bible forgotten, faith in God nebulous, no more sacred music, a literature from which has been deleted the ideas and ideals that have their roots in the Bible . . . let all that happen, then see the ultimate end of *no churches.*

Do we want that, any of us? I don't. I doubt you do. If you feel that in a real sense you do not want to live without the church, if you do not want it to go out of existence, take this as an invitation to take the first step that takes you toward the Christian fellowship that is the church.

Let's imagine a conversation: In the year A.D. 90, Shimon Maburak said, "For many reasons these are difficult days in which to hold the Christian faith. The major events of our time are so essentially anti-Christian that against their background Christian faith seems to be mere wistful thinking, a pleasant utopian dream."

Today we hear the same thing. Indeed Christianity's very desirability is used as an argument againt it. Granted, Christian faith is comforting, sustaining, brings solace and encouragement to those in trouble. That is precisely the reason Christian faith has developed, say its critics; not because it is objectively true but because it is subjectively comfortable. In one book after another we are told that Christian faith is a lovely fantasy, creating a world of make-believe where people up against cruel reality find encouragement by fooling themselves. As a character in a novel put it, "There is something about a church. . . . There's beauty in it . . . it's a pleasant drug."

To be sure, Christian faith is desirable because it is comforting, encouraging, and reassuring. That is one reason. It is not the only reason people are religious. The stark facts of this harsh universe and the dreadful ills of human life are insupportable for many among us unless they are concealed, dressed up, and decorated in some comforting faith. Another fictional character was made to say, "Land sakes! I don't see how people live at all who don't cheer themselves up by thinkin' of God and heaven."

Such a statement causes some to say that Christian faith is an illusion, that it does not face reality. As one cynic said, "Religion is nothing more than a chloroform mask into which the weak and unhappy stick their faces."

Over against such a view, prevalent since Shimon's time, I put the testimony of the New Testament. Tell that to those first-century Christians. They were not evading anything. Theirs was no illusionary living. They were up against some harsh realities.

One of the most extraordinary eras in human history was the first century of the Christian movement. Our calendars are dated from its beginning. Any way one looks at it, it was an amazing turning point in humanity's journey. The most amazing thing of all is the ordinary character of most of the people who helped lead mankind around that corner. Let's have no romantic illusions about them. The New Testament is realistically honest about those early Christians. It speaks of their cruelty, slowness of comprehension, prejudices, self-seeking, and twisting of doctrine. And yet those were men and women who helped inaugurate one of the great new eras of human history.

In the preface to *Pilgrim's Progress*, John Bunyan explains that he was drawn into writing the allegory when he was occupied with another book.

> I had undertook
> To make another, which when almost done,
> Before I was aware, I this begun.

The writer of the Epistle of Jude had the same experience. He evidently wanted to write something to solidify the common experience shared by those early Christians. Instead, he wrote an appeal to defend the faith against some whose heretical beliefs and immoral behavior were a threatening menace. They had infiltrated the Christian community. They denied Jesus Christ and perverted the grace of God into licentiousness. Jude never tells us the belief or practices of those heretics. It is always easier to condemn conduct than to refute ideas. So he denounces rather than describes.

The major tenet of any religious faith, and especially the Judeo-Christian faith, is the assertion that this fugitive earthly scene is permeated by something eternal, that transciency is not the last word in this universe, that life's changefulness is saturated with an unchanging purpose, and that behind and within all "from everlasting to everlasting" is God. For those distraught with life's uncertainties, Christian faith has certainty to offer, not by denying life's transciency, but by asserting the eternal. When everything that can teeter is tottering, that is the time for us to seek and see what stands firm.

The writer of Jude spoke about a "faith which was once for all delivered" (verse 3). The writer of the Epistle to the Hebrews spoke of "Jesus Christ . . . the same yesterday and today and forever" (Hebrews 13:8). Both of them wrote during a time when life was being shaken, when people needed something to hold on to. But it was *faith*, not specifics about faith, and it was faith in God. The truths of Jesus Christ may be always the same, but societies change.

In Shakespeare's plays, for example, we can see customs, circumstances, and ways of thinking and speaking so at variance with ours that they loudly call attention to how human life changes. Then come to those passages that have no date: Hamlet facing indecision, Lady MacBeth wrestling with guilt-remorse, Portia pleading for mercy. The centuries vanish, and we confront the timeless, ageless, dateless soul of humankind.

From work or church we go to our homes by bus or automobile. Each is relatively new. The gadgets with which our homes are equipped are new. But read Homer's *Odys-*

sey and listen to this: "There is nothing mightier or nobler than when man and wife are of one heart and mind in a house." Some things are eternal: truth, purpose, moral law, and human personality.

Of course truth is not an exclusive of Christian faith, but at least Christians ought to be aware of Eternal Truth, wherever it comes from. Truth is not always a visible, tangible thing. Sometimes it moves on a level not to be seen, touched, weighed, or measured.

A story is told of a lad whose father had long been away from home as a hostage of war. One day, standing in front of a picture of his father, the lad said to his mother, "I wish Dad could step out of that frame."

As Christian faith sees it, God stepped out of the frame and in Jesus Christ made Himself known. John said, "The Word became flesh and dwelt among us" (John 1:14). Paul said, "God was in Christ" (2 Corinthians 5:19). The Christian faith looks upon an obscure Man from Galilee, whose family thought him demented, whose church excommunicated him for heresy, whose friends thought him a failure, and whose government crucified him as a traitor . . . and believe that God was in him. All this sounds incredible, but that's where we stand. Jesus Christ is the center of our faith, however we define that faith. He stands as the central personality revealing God, however we believe that. We begin with God and end with Jesus, or we start with Jesus and find God. After that, what do we do, what have we done?

In the main, there are two ways by which to gain the allegiance of people: bribe them with some enticement, or challenge them with some dream. Let no one ever say that Jesus got his followers on false pretenses. He told people bluntly what would be in store for them if they joined up with him. His was a realism with no evasions. No rewards were promised during the journey. Instead they were told to count the cost from the beginning.

We may appeal to the selfish instinct in every person and make some "rice Christians," as some early missionaries were accused of doing. Bribe, and we get lip-time service and when the storms of life hit there are many defectors. Or we may appeal to the heroic instinct and capture the imagination, as the church has often done. Challenge, and those who respond will proffer the utmost in love and loyalty. Jesus knew that. With him it was never a bribe but always a challenge. This is not to say that he was always successful. He wasn't. Some who responded to the challenge fell by the way. Some Christians today aren't always ready for the problems.

We make a colossal mistake if we think we can casually saunter along the Christian way, hands swinging, hips swaying, whistling a merry tune. Christian discipleship is not what some seem to think it is—a sort of pastime which one happens to be caught up in, something to be taken up and put down at will according to inclination.

It meant something and it cost something to be a Christian in those first years. No one from A.D. 30 to A.D. 300 thought of Christianity as being comfortable. Christianity was associated with troublemakers and persecution. It was a way of life that called for a dedication that would test not only their faith but their endurance. Not all of those early Christians were heroic souls. For the most part, they were people like us. Some of the things they did and some of the methods they used were abhorrent and less than Christian. But at their best they were heroic. History has repeated their faults and their victories.

It is easy to look at Jesus as a meek and gentle man, a sensitive idealist who told marvelous stories and went about doing good things. This Jesus appeals to us. On the other hand, he went about giving offense to his relatives, the religious leaders, people with vested interests, and the politicians. He said that he had come to cast fire upon the earth and that he brought not peace but a sword. This side of Jesus doesn't have as much appeal to us. However, we can't dismiss it. We may prefer to emphasize one side more than the other, and some still do, but both are there. We may find peace and comfort in the gently sensitive Jesus, but we dare not overlook those stern elements in his character and message.

Jesus challenged, dared, and made life demanding and awesome. He would have no headstrong enlistees, no impulsive converts, no hesitant followers. It was not that he didn't want disciples. He did. Rather, he wanted dependable disciples who would volunteer for the duration. He had some failures. He sometimes took less than he wanted in the hope that they would develop. Judas was one who defected. Peter was accepted on less terms than full commitment, but Peter came on to give it everything he had.

Here is where Jesus bothers us today. Some do reject him because they do not understand him. But I should think that more reject him because they understand him only too well. They know his demands are stern and strict, and they are not quite prepared for that.

This is not to fuss at anyone, for I include myself in all this. Along with those dedicated, disciplined disciples who have changed the course of history, there have been more of us who believe and desire, but can't be quite as committed as Paul, or Luther, or Wesley. We are in the Christian way of life—if not in midstream, at least on the edge with a foot in the water. We have made a beginning. Now we are to work on understanding, devotion, and dedication and hope to make some progress.

Perhaps many of us do look at being a Christian in rather easy terms, feeling that God is always next door, available. But we also know that life's journey is perilous with its windings and turnings, its ups and downs, and God is with us in all that. The way is narrower and straighter than we would like. But at least we've begun the journey. To others we would say, "Come on along. Edge on in, if that's as much as you can do. But make a start."

As I recall, Henry Ward Beecher once said, "Religion means work. Religion means work in a dirty world. Religion means peril; blows given, but blows taken as well. Religion means transformation. The world is to be cleaned up by somebody; and you are not called by God if you are ashamed to scour and scrub."

Liberal Christians have been accused of thinning down Christian belief. In trying to formulate our Christian faith into credible forms there is some danger of that. We have to rid ourselves of some incredible beliefs and theologies that make consent to Christian faith either insincere or impossible. Instead of thinning down, I would use the cooking term "reducing" where by boiling a sauce or liquid over high heat it is reduced in volume, generally by half. The result is a rich and savory concentration.

There is something wildly exciting about staking one's life on God. Against all that is dark and damnable in life, faith in God risks everything on what is right. What is courage? Courage is staking life on a possibility. What is faith? Faith is believing that the possibility really exists. Such was the venturesome faith that carried Jesus to and through the cross. Let us never think that majestic faith is something easy. Let us not seek something easy to believe. Rather let us seek for something great to believe and then do.

Thoughtful observers of man's moral conduct have always been concerned about the dangers of gambling. To have ingrained in one's thinking and dominant in one's living the idea that some day we may succeed by chance in getting something for nothing is about as disastrous to moral integrity as any evil that can beset a person. Yet gambling seems to be ingrained in us. In most respects, every man is a gambler. Whatever achievement we seek, we have to hazard our lives on something or other. Everyone of us wagers our effort on some uncertainty every day we live. Here is a strange, intriguing aspect of human existence. Life is not simply a game of chance, it is more that that, but one cannot understand it without taking into account this element of risk. To some extent, we are gamblers . . . all of us.

Even the scene on Calvary illustrates this. At the foot of the cross the soldiers are gambling for Jesus' robe. But as they cast their dice, see what Jesus is doing on the cross. G. A. Studdert-Kennedy, a British chaplain-poet of World War I, put it this way:

> And sitting down they watched Him there,
> The soldiers did.
> There, while they played with dice,
> He made His sacrifice,
> And died upon the Cross to rid
> God's world of sin.
> He was a gambler, too,
> My Christ,
> He took his life and threw
> It for a world redeemed.
> And ere His agony was done,
> Before the westering sun went down,
> Crowning that day with its crimson crown,
> He knew
> That He had won.[2]

There was gambling that day not only at the foot of the cross, but on it.

> He took his life and threw
> It for a world redeemed.

---

[2]*The Sorrows of God and Other Poems* (New York: G. H. Doran, 1924).

We may get weary of hearing about and living in the midst of uncertainties. What is going to happen to us? We don't know. How can we tell what good or evil will fall upon the people and things we love and care most about? We can't.

Our characters and our careers are determined largely by things on which we wager our lives. Life is a continuous adventure into the unforeseen and unforeseeable. We must find out, if we can, what ideas and ideals, what aims and purposes, what manner and philosophy of living on which we are to risk our lives. Bluntly, on what are we going to bet our lives?

The thrill and excitement of life rises at this very point. Granted that the necessity of risking life in the midst of un-certainties grows wearisome. We become tired of our unknown tomorrows and cry not for excitement but for safety. If we could just have a little time of security or certainty, some bit of release from risk . . . a lifetime, no-cut contract.

Yet life with its risks and hazards gone and everything reduced to certainty would be intolerably dull. To know in advance everything that would happen to us, our loved ones, our world this year and the next . . . how insuffera-bly boring. Should we find ourselves in such a circum-stance we would cry for the old uncertainties. "God," we would pray, "let us risk it again. It was better that way."

A prayer of Francis G. Peabody begins, "Make us ready for the great adventure of living. We do not pray for im-munity from risks; we pray for courage to face risks."

You may not expect a Christian preacher to say a good word in favor of high stakes for great winnings in the world's most exciting and important game— *life*. But I am. We are wagering our lives on something good or bad, high or low. And whatever it is we are staking our lives upon will be our making or our ruin.

Faith is an essential part of our intellectual apparatus.

Knowledge is what is behind us, what has brought us to where we are. Faith is the capacity to risk our lives on something as we move into the unknown beyond where we are. Faith requires that we take a dim view of the present only because we hold a bright view of the future. Faith arouses, as nothing else can, a fervor for the possible.

Looking at and understanding faith that way, one wishes we had more of it in our religion. How many people, when they think of "Christian faith," think of some creed? The trouble with a creed is not simply that it becomes a rigid form of regimentation. The trouble is rather that a creed tends to make Chrstianity something finished, its ideas set, and so makes faith in Jesus Christ something dull and gives consent to a static formula. Nothing could be farther from the truth.

Christianity is the hazarding of a great faith in God and a great hope for man. Christianity lives on a frontier. What has been thought and done is behind us. We learn from that. What is to be thought and done lies ahead of us. That is the call of faith for volunteers to stake their lives on following this Jesus of Nazareth.

We cannot remain neutral. We cannot move through life betting our life on nothing. We may say we cannot make up our minds, but we cannot avoid making up our *lives*. That gets made up for us one way or the other because deep inside we wager our lives on something. I plead for higher stakes on great issues. Above all, for someone who will take his/her life and throw it for a world redeemed.

There was a seventh-century Christian philosopher-scientist named Blaise Pascal who said, "Either God exists or He does not exist. So why not gamble. Place a wager, bet that God exists. If you gain, you gain everything; if you lose, you lose nothing. Wager, then, without hesitation, that He exists."

† This Life, Then Death: Is That All There Is?

The time comes when we must face up to our mortality—the fact that we are going to die, that life is a terminal disease.

One time in a conversation with a friend, I said, "Myron, you and I both think we shall become the second Enoch. The thing is, you only *think* you will be while I *know* I will. But there is that nagging suspicion that we may both be wrong."

He chuckled, and said, "Avery, I *know* you are wrong."

In an article on the life and career of actor Yul Brynner, a sentence was attributed to him that he said came from his Gypsy heritage: "Your life is getting shorter." I like that. At my age, I *know* that. I believe I have a realistic concept of death, and have come to terms with my own mortality. But is there anything beyond death? Or is this life all there is? Either way doesn't bother me. I want to believe that there is some kind of life beyond this earthly existence, *and I do.* There is good "liberal" Christian company in this belief: Harry Emerson Fosdick and Leslie D. Weatherhead, for example.

The religions of the world, from primitive to more sophisticated, teach that this life is a part of a much larger existence that goes beyond our earthly life span. Such belief is not ruled out by any established scientific findings or by any agreed philosophical arguments. I believe this basic religious teaching is true, although it cannot be proved.It is a matter of faith.

To talk about heaven or immortality (henceforth the words shall be used interchangeably) we must talk about death. No one likes to do that. We are reluctant even to speak the word *death.* Instead, we use such euphemisms as "expired" (a favorite around hospitals) or "passed on." Occasionally we may say "deceased," but seldom do we say *died.*

Humanly speaking, I don't like anything about death. It cuts off loved ones, breaks up homes, destroys friendships, and wrecks careers. Death causes sorrow, produces pain, and brings grief. The only good thing to be said is that it sometimes brings release from much physical suffering and pain. It is from the Christian point of view that death makes any sense at all, for the Christian faith sings, "Death has no more dominion over us."

One of the first sermons I ever preached—the third, to be exact—dealt with the theme of the immortality of the soul. Who was I, an inexperienced high school senior, to be dealing with so grand a theme? Yet, why not? Teenagers do think about death. Read their poetry efforts. My wife teaches French in one of the finest private schools in the nation. Quite often, when she assigns them compositions, her students discuss death. She lets me read some of them. Well, she translates, for I can't read French. Those intelligent, sophisticated high schoolers have some exquisite thoughts.

I don't know that I have anything more specific to say now than was said in that early sermon, except that I have had five decades of experience, training, study, and thought to refine what was said. The conclusions—which those years ago I took on simple faith from others—are now my own conclusions, which have come out of some tough personal experience.

I've gone through the place that not only wonders, but borders close on saying that when this life of ours ceases, that's all there is to it. But this kind of attitude ends in a despair expressed in the statement of an earlier generation and revived in our own time: "There is no reason for life and life has no meaning."

This attitude caused Pulitzer-prize-winning dramatist Tennessee Williams to have Big Daddy say in *Cat on a Hot Tin Roof*, "When you're gone from here, boy, you are long gone and nowhere. The human machine is no different from the animal machine or the fish machine or the reptile machine or the insect machine."

I've toyed with that but could never bring myself to take that plunge. Something within me has always rebelled at that outlook. Call it what you will, but I prefer to say it is because of a basic belief in God.

I've gone through the mood of thinking that the desire for personal immortality may be ridiculously egotistical. Why should we be so selfish as to look forward to a future world in which we shall be rewarded for being good? Why not do right and be good because *it is right* instead of doing so for a reward?

In one of his essays, Montaigne said, "Even if I should not follow the straight road because of its straightness, I would follow it because I have found by experience that when all is said and done it is generally the happiest and the most useful." He elaborated with the figure of a sailor and his rudder:

> The mariner of old said thus to Neptune in a great tempest. "O God! thou mayest save me if thou wilt, and if thou wilt, thou mayest destroy me; but whether or no, I will steer my rudder true."[1]

That—holding one's rudder true—is a far nobler motive for right living than a heavenly reward. And my rudder has often slipped.

A hymn attributed to Francis Xavier, a sixteenth-century Catholic missionary to the Orient, expresses a similar sentiment:

> My God, I love thee,
>   not because I hope for heaven thereby,
> Not with hope of gaining aught,
> Not seeking a reward,
> But as thyself hast loved me, O everloving Lord!
> E'en so I love thee, and will love,
> And in thy Praise will sing,
> Solely because thou art my God, and my eternal King.

I know the moods of asking why should we desire another life, anyway: why not quit worrying about another life and make something worthwhile out of this one? Most of the conventional pictures of what Reinhold Niebuhr called "the furniture of heaven and the temperature of hell" have left me emotionless.

I mention these things because you've passed through them also. Oh, we haven't really adopted them, you and I, but we have toyed with them. Maybe we haven't shouted such ideas aloud, but they are familiar to us. Most of us have

---

[1]Michel Eyquem de Montaigne, *Essays*, bk. 2, chap. 16.

a queer inner feeling that we human beings were meant for more than just a few brief years upon the planet Earth and then a passing into nothingness. The mysterious force that makes this universe tick is throbbing with life. And we feel that throb. It surges deep within us. It pulsates as strong as the steady thump of the pulse at our wrist.

Even the playwright Tennessee Williams feels a bit of that throb, for he has Big Daddy say in another place, while talking about tourists in Europe, "The reason he buys everything he can buy is that in the back of his mind he has the crazy hope that one of his purchases will be life everlasting—which it can never be."

We may not be able to express our feelings as movingly as the poet, or as dramatically as the playwright, or as strongly as the theologian, but we have them.

In Wordsworth's lovely "Ode" with the clumsy subtitle "Intimations of Immortality from Recollections of Early Childhood," there are some exquisite lines (lines 58-66, 162-68):

> Our birth is but a sleep and a forgetting:
> The Soul that rises with us, our life's Star,
>   Hath had elsewhere in its setting,
>   And cometh from afar:
>   Not in entire forgetfulness,
>   And not in utter nakedness,
> But trailing clouds of glory do we come
>   From God, who is our home:
> Heaven lies about us in our infancy!
>
> . . . .
>
>   Hence in a season of calm weather
>   Though inland far we be,
> Our Souls have sight of that immortal sea
>   Which brought us hither,
>   Can in a moment travel thither,
> And see the Children sport upon the shore,

And hear the mighty waters rolling evermore.

Get the beauty of those lines by reading them again: "Our life's star . . . cometh from afar . . . Not in entire forgetfulness . . . But trailing clouds of glory do we come from God, who is our home . . . Our souls have sight of that immortal sea."

We do belong to eternity. Our life had its birth there. It is there we must return.

Let me quote Tennessee Williams again, this time to let Big Mama speak: "Time goes by so fast. Nothin' can outrun it. Death commences too early—almost before you're half acquainted with life you meet the other."

Death shocks us. Everywhere we go we are engaged in a continuous battle with this enemy. Wherever we go we find people in pursuit of plans for keeping alive. Even those who say that death is God's will, will fight God's will with every possible measure. And, why not fight death? Manna Zucca sings,

> I love life, so I want to live,
> To drink of life's fullness, take all it can give.

You and I sing the same song.

This constant struggle is due to two things: first, the feeling that death is the termination, the end, long-gone, so we want as much life as we can have; second, the feeling that there is more to life than death, so we want this life to prepare for that more. And we get so involved in the tension of these two extremes that we don't quite know what to do.

We talk about the terrible waste of which we Americans are so guilty in connection with the natural resources of this country. We *are* wasteful. But if death ends all, then of all wasters, God would be the worst. He would produce lives and throw them away as finished. He would create capacities never used and possibilities unfilled. He would take the most valuable thing we know—human personality—and leave it as unfinished business.

We face immense difficulties in discussing immortality. It is a mystery too deep for us. Nothing we can say, no word picture we may paint is adequate. There is no proof. We believe or we do not believe. Remember Wordsworth's line: "Our birth is but a sleep and a forgetting." We are like unborn babies in a mother's womb. What faces the unborn is not death, but birth, though that birth does terminate one form of life. It is birth into an unknown world, not a single detail of which the unborn can imagine.

> What no eye has seen, nor ear heard,
> nor the heart of man conceived,
> what God has prepared for those who love him. . . .
> —1 Corinthians 2:9

Paul is right about that. Paul is also right about "This mortal must put on immortality" (1 Corinthians 15:53-54). For God is not the God of unfinished business, nor is God a waster.

What if we did resign ourselves to an ultimate meaninglessness of life? To be sure, there would be some noble souls who would go on trying to live good lives for good causes, holding their rudder true. I know some who do not believe in immortality who are living magnificent lives of unselfish service. My closest friend is such a person. But I submit that such lives are sustained by the faith of millions who are so sure that life is worthwhile that it is to be forever. The very idea that every human personality is sacred is rooted in such soil. The idea of the value of human life, the dignity of man, depends upon such belief. Otherwise, human life is valueless, meaningless, and deserves to end. The idea of man's worth, and that good things are to be done with life, would soon be gone if we took away all belief in immortality.

Scientists tell us that it was change in the physical climate and environment that got rid of dinosaurs and monstrous reptiles which once roamed the earth. Well, change the spiritual and moral climate by removing man's worth and dignity, remove the idea of immortality, and the finest qualities of humanity will disappear.

Why is it we are so torn to pieces by death? Because it upsets our plans, cuts into our emotions, ruins our ambitions, leaves unfinished business, and causes sorrow. Yes, all of that. But the more basic reason is love, love for people; more specifically, love for a person, *one person*.

Plato's *Phaedo* is one of the finest arguments for immortality in the ancient world. But Plato and his friends were not thinking about themselves, but about Socrates whom they loved. *Death ought not to be the end of him!*

The New Testament is radiant with hope about eternal life. But the disciples, more than thinking about themselves, were saying about Jesus that death had no dominion over him, thus there was hope for them.

When faith in immortality rises strong and confident, its source is not egotism, but love; love not so much directed toward desires for one's own eternal life, but for that of another.

In his "In Memoriam A. H. H.," Tennyson said,

> Thou wilt not leave us in the dust:
>   Thou madest man, he knows not why,
>   He thinks he was not made to die;
> And Thou hast made him: thou are just.

because Tennyson cared so much for his friend, Arthur Henry Hallam.

In "Threnody," Ralph Waldo Emerson affirmed that

> . . . What is excellent,

As God lives, is permanent;
Hearts are dust, hearts' loves remain;
Heart's love will meet thee again.

because he cared so deeply for his little son Waldo who had died.

For the Christian, death is not the end. It is the beginning of more meaningful life. Why? Because God loves us and cares enough for us (at a deeper level than Plato or Tennyson or Emerson) that He wants more life for us. That is, for the Christian—other than the sense of personal loss—death is not the mournful thing we make it. It is a time of rejoicing. That's what Paul said it was: "To depart and be with Christ is far better" (Philippians 1:23).

It is we who remain who sorrow. When Jesus Christ is the center of our lives, then it is better to depart, for death becomes the portal through which we pass into the larger life with God, whatever that life may be. Paraphrasing Wordsworth, "Death becomes a sleep and a forgetting."

The Bible does not seek to prove eternal life (immortality). That can't be done. Such a belief is the consequence of belief in God. We decide for ourselves whether the greatest expert on religious matters, Jesus of Nazareth, was right or wrong. If we decide Jesus was right, we approach death with the same confidence with which we approach life. As life has meaning and purpose, so does death. The Bible recognizes the reality of death. We must realize that one day we, our loved ones, and our friends are going to die. The Bible looks this fact squarely in the eye; so must we. We must face it realistically.

Eternal life is the gift of God, not something we *earn*. We may want it, but we cannot demand it. The Bible describes eternal life as *rebirth*. As a grain of wheat must die before it is reborn, so must we. Even in this life we put off the old in order to put on the new.

Actually, the Bible does not understand eternal life as

something that begins when we die. Such life is possible here and now. To the degree that our lives are wrapped up in God, oriented toward Jesus Christ, we are living eternally. We experience in fragmentary form the quality of life that is deathless. This kind of life is not terminated by death. Rather, death is the release for the highest quality of life in fellowship with God. What this involves is preparation. This life is to be lived so that it will have a foundation to cushion the shock of losing a loved one. Without such preparation, no wonder so many go to pieces.

Thornton Wilder gives us a beautiful confession of faith. In *Our Town*, he says,

> I don't care what they say with their mouths—everybody knows that *something* is eternal. And it ain't houses, and it ain't even stars—everybody knows in their bones that *something* is eternal, and that something has to do with human beings. And all the greatest people ever lived have been telling us that for five thousand years and yet you'd be surprised how people are always losing hold of it. There's something way down deep that's eternal about every human being.

For the Christian, death doesn't end everything. For the still-living Christian, death doesn't end everything, although some seem to think so. Life goes on. It can still be good, beautiful, and meaningful—depending on what we make of it, how we face it, whether we believe that God can still allow us to have some heaven on earth as well as for eternity.

Here I am, seventy-five years old. There's not much time left for me. A few months, perhaps a decade or more. Who knows? I can say that I've enjoyed it. Life has been good, despite the traumas, heartaches, and pain. I believe in God and that God loves me. There are many acquaintances and a few close friends. I have been privileged to love and be loved in return. There has been a sense of purpose in what I've done, not always at my best. Whatever may lie beyond will also be good—different, but good. If there is nothing more, if this life is all there is, so what! I don't know much about what I've been saying, but I believe what I've been talking about. I need to say what that man said to Jesus: "I believe; help my unbelief!" (Mark 9:24).

In any discussion of life after death, one must look at the opposite of heaven . . . hell. (Why is it we say we *go* to heaven, but are *sent* to hell?) As to whether hell is fiction or fact, I don't know. I don't stand in the hellfire, brimstone, damnation tradition. The idea of grinning little devils with pitchforks and burning fire is dependent upon Dante, Milton, and Michelangelo, not the Bible.

Consider the following regarding the meaning of hell.

> Hell really means unfitness for heaven. Hell is the consequence of a way of life and a kind of self-training which utterly and radically unfits a man for such satisfactions as heaven provides, a way of life which so emphasizes man's own individuality, so blinds him in the fog of self-love, that he is incapable of the worship of God or of unselfish living in community with his fellow creatures. Hell is the opposite of heaven. It is the fruit of a human existence which has rejected God and the worship of God and society as a sphere of service. From such a life there comes a final and ultimate failure to attain the true destiny of human nature in heaven, and this final failure to attain true destiny the Bible calls hell.[2]

There are three major words in the Bible that we translate as "hell." One of those words is "Gehenna," from *ge-*

---

[2]George W. Barrett and J. V. Langmeade Casserley, *Dialogue on Destiny* (Greenwich CT: Seabury Press, 1955) 68.

hinnom, the Hebrew name for the Valley of Hinnom at Jerusalem, a place where refuse was taken, dumped, and burned. It has become a definite place with a fixed purpose. (Actually, refuse was dumped and burned in the Valley of Hinnom, just outside the old walls of Jerusalem, as late as the Arab control of old Jerusalem. The Israelis stopped this practice after the 1967 war.)

The other two words are "Sheol," the Old Testament word for the realm of the dead, with Hades as its New Testament Greek equivalent. Sheol is referred to as a place, a region of darkness, a place of privation, and a place of separation, especially from God. In the Old Testament the picture of Sheol is as a place where men hover around like fleeting shadows. The bad thing about Sheol, in the biblical sense, is that the dead can no longer praise God. They can no longer see His face. They can no longer take part in the Sabbath services. It is a state of exclusion from God. And that is what makes death so fearful and hell what it is—exclusion from God.

The imagination of a believer in God may not be adequate to comprehend existence apart from God. Godlessness, the opposite of godliness, is existence apart from God. What else but separation is left to us as a result of unbelief? It is certainly not God's will that we perish. We bring that on ourselves when we insist on our own way. So we are left to one little corner of the universe which we call our own, and in which we may live as if God did not exist.

Hell cannot merely be shrugged off as an antiquated concept that has no meaning for twentieth-century sophisticates. To be in hell—or whatever equivalent term we use—is to be a derelict in a wasteland where God is absent, where there is no exit marked "This Way Out." Nor is there a signpost directing us to God. Why is it that most of what we read or hear from those who feel themselves in some slough of despond, their own hell, do not describe the experience in terms of intense heat, but rather speak of the cold clamminess of isolated desolation? I submit that it is due to the absence of hope: there seems to be no way out. For them, God is absent.

Let's take this idea of separation a bit further. We can figure distances in mileage and know how far apart we are. To be absent from a loved one, either by a continent or a world, is not easy. But physical distance is lessened by the knowledge that we can get together in a matter of hours if necessary. Physical distance is nothing to compare with another kind of separation. We may live in the same house or be in the same room with another person and feel farther apart than the physical distance of thousands of miles. And *that is hell.*

Separation is a moral principle. We are separated in nature and purpose. Our will is set against the will of another. As Isaiah put it,

> Your iniquities have made a separation
>   between you and your God,
> and your sins have hid his face from you
>   so that he does not hear.   —Isaiah 59:2

A character in T. S. Eliot's *Cocktail Party* puts it this way:

Hell is oneself. Hell is alone, the other figures in it merely projections. There is nothing to escape from and nothing to escape to. One is always alone.

Even simpler are the words of William Morris:

Fellowship is life, and lack of fellowship is death;
fellowship is heaven, and lack of fellowship is hell.

In all this, are we to say that hell is endless, forever, everlasting? In the main, Christianity answers in the affirmative. But at all stages of history there have been dissenting voices, protesting that God's love is all enduring, and that he will never cease his efforts to win every person to himself. Perhaps even in hell God is at work, and one by one souls are wooed out of that place. I don't know. But we dare not assume that everyone will respond, even then, for the armor of self-centeredness is sometimes so hard that no love or kindness can pierce it.

In the 19 May 1967 issue of *Time* magazine the "Religion" section had a lot to say on this subject. *Time* quoted Jewish rabbis, Roman Catholic priests, and Protestant clergy who rejected any idea of hell at all, much less make it everlasting. Most of the men quoted took the position called "Universalism." That is, God's salvation is universal and no one will be forever condemned to hell. Two quotations will suffice here:

> Man in his totality was created and will be saved.
> —Peter Riga,
> Roman Catholic, St. Mary's College, California

> If God is a God of love, if he is ultimate, that which he loves and sustains he will not simply discard.
> —Robert McAfee Brown,
> Presbyterian, Stanford University

I must confess that this position has a strong appeal for me. Yet although I like the idea and want to accept it, I have not been quite able to go all the way. I see no biblical teaching of any kind of "purgatory," whether we call it that or not. There are four major statements in making the case for universalism:

1. Punishment is intended to make the wrong-doer a right-doer. (This is true, and it often works out that way, but not always—certainly not in our penal systems.)
2. No earthly parent, or society, practices everlasting punishment. (But there are some parents who disown their

children, and many societies practice life imprisonment or capital punishment.)
3. Even in life after death the power of choice remains. If the soul remains a soul, it retains the power of choice. (I would agree. But there is also the possibility for the choice to remain negative. If we grant the possibility of repentance after death, escaping hell, would we go so far as to say there is the possibility of losing heaven, that is, denying God after death?)
4. Jesus Christ is never satisfied with ninety-nine percent. So long as one sheep is lost in the wilderness, the Good Shepherd is concerned with that one sheep's safety. (Granted, but that one sheep can still be willfully disobedient.)

George B. Caird wrote the volume on Revelation in the Harper Bible Commentary. His position on universal salvation may be summarized as follows: "Hell is God's last tribute to the dignity of man. God respects us enough to allow us the final choice to self-destruct."

Gian Carlo Menotti, the modern Italian-American composer of such operas as *The Saints of Bleecker Street,* has this definition:

> Hell begins on the day when God grants us a clear vision of all that we might have achieved, of all the gifts we have wasted, of all that we might have done that we did not do. . . . For me the conception of hell lies in two words: "Too late."

None of this need be that way, not according to Christian faith. At the heart of the Christian gospel is the proclamation of God's forgiving love, that hell need not be for us, that we need not be separated, that there is a chance to begin again, that we may be in eternal fellowship with God.

✝ A Sermon

The Impossible Dream

Most of the sermons a preacher delivers are quickly forgotten. Many of them should be. Perhaps some should have never been offered. Some fifty years ago some famous preachers were asked to submit one sermon for a collection entitled *If I Had But One Sermon to Preach*. Were I asked to do a similar thing, this sermon is what I would submit. It was first delivered at the St. Charles Avenue Baptist Church in New Orleans, 22 September 1968. It was repeated each year through 1980, when I retired. Then it became my first sermon at the University Baptist Church in Hattiesburg, Mississippi, and was repeated each anniversary and as the retirement sermon in 1985. In addition it has been used other places. Each time it was essentially the same, with a different introduction and some variations to meet the current situation. It summarizes my outlook, attitude, and philosophy.

† † †

When Dale Wasserman's multi-prize-winning musical play, *Man of La Mancha*, was seeking producers and financial backing in 1966 it had great difficulty because it was regarded as too intellectual and too idealistic. That was the time of beginning disillusion about Viet Nam, the hippie culture, riots, burnings, lootings, and an antiestablishment attitude that included rejecting the church. People, particularly youth, were trying to break away from home, whatever home was. The play was plowing squarely upstream against the prevailing philosophy of so-called realism in the theater. It was a realism called by such names as Theater of the Absurd, Theater of Black Comedy, Theater of Cruelty. The realism dealt with a variety of sexual perversions, emphasizing the sordid side of life. I know, of course, that there are sexual perversions and some of life is mean and low. Some people do live that way.

Were this same play seeking producers and financial backing today, I rather think it would have the same difficulty, for it goes against our self-centered complacency. People today are unsure of themselves, scared of the future, and looking for security. The church is something to be taken or left alone. Parents in the past two decades have been so unsure of their own values and goals that they have been unable to pass values and goals on to their children. Fathers are too busy trying to make money and mothers are too busy trying to find themselves. Children have been raised as if an experiment in chemistry were being conducted, tentatively mixing in this ingredient and that one, hoping for some success, but fearing the whole thing will blow up in their faces.

But I am convinced that neither the thumbing of the nose at all establishments, including the church, nor the self-centered search that ignores the church is the true realism of life; that many people do not live that way; that life is basically good; and that most people, in their own little way, are trying to make it better.

Man of La Mancha is an effort to stress the quality of life that looks for and emphasizes the best of life. Albert Marre, who produced the play, watched the show and audience reactions night after night, and said, "They're not just watching a play, they're having a religious experience."

That is what it was for me the first time I saw the play: *a religious experience.*

The story is about Don Quixote, that exciting character of fiction created by Miguel de Cervantes, who dared to attempt the absurd in order to achieve the impossible. Dale Wasserman, who wrote the play, deserves credit for calling us back to the reality of dreaming impossible dreams, of looking for and seeing the best qualities in our fellow men, and of having ideals toward which we strive, even if we don't reach them.

Listen to a few samples from the play's dialogue. Of himself, Cervantes says,

> It is true that I am guilty of these charges. An idealist? Well, I have never had the courage to believe in nothing.

In describing how Don Quixote came into being:

> Being retired, he has much time for books. He studies them from morn till night. . . . And all he reads oppresses him . . . fills him with indignation at man's murderous ways toward man. He broods . . . and broods . . . and broods—and finally from so much brooding his brains dry up! He lays down the melancholy burden of sanity and conceives the strangest project ever imagined . . . to become a knight-errant and sally forth into the world to right all wrongs.

Aldonza, the female lead, is described as "a savage, dark alley cat, survivor if not always victor of many back-fence tussles." But Don Quixote sees her as his lady fair and sings,

I see heaven when I see thee, Dulcinea,
And thy name is like a prayer an angel whispers. . . .
Dulcinea . . . Dulcinea.

The Padre says of Quixote,

There is either the wisest madman or the maddest wise man in the world.

But Quioxte says that the important thing for him in life is "Only that I follow the quest." Then he sings that beautiful song, "The Impossible Dream."

Aldonza, trying to get him to come off the Dulcinea bit, says, "Once—just once—would you look at me as I really am?"

And Quixote replies, "I see beauty. Purity. I see the woman each man holds secret within him. Dulcinea."

Two more quotations for the present. The Duke says, "A man must come to terms with life as it is."

And Cervantes answers,

When life itself seems lunatic, who knows where madness lies? Perhaps to be too practical is madness. To surrender dreams—this may be madness. To seek treasure where there is only trash. Too much sanity may be madness. And maddest of all, *to see life as it is and not as it should be.* (Italics mine.)

Out of his frustration and bitterness as a Negro poet in an earlier generation, Langston Hughes posed one of life's most haunting questions:

What happens to a dream deferred?

> Does it dry up
> like a raisin in the sun?
> Or fester like a sore—
> And then run?
> Does it stink like rotten meat?
> Or crust and sugar over—
> like a syrupy sweet?
>
> Maybe it just sags
> like a heavy load.
>
> *Or does it explode?*   —"Harlem" (1951)

This is one of the pivotal questions now troubling the American—*and the Christian*—conscience. What does happen to a dream deferred?

In the public sector we live with the politics of postponement. Political promises unfulfilled have caused the disenfranchised at home and abroad to grow increasingly restless as the prize that once seemed within grasp recedes farther away. Martin Luther King, Jr.'s, phrase, "I have a Dream," which speaks for us all, has become a caterwauling chorus of, "God, what a nightmare!"

Ancient Israel was a people founded on a dream, on a promise given to a man named Abraham. The story is too long to retell here. The reminder that this is the story of the Bible is enough. A band of rebels, an outfit of slaves, led by a fugitive from Egyptian justice named Moses, started toward a Promised Land. They finally forged themselves into a nation in an area no larger than Louisiana, sandwiched between a seacoast on the west with no harbors and a desert on the east with no highways. The mighty armies of their neighbors marched back and forth across that land as constant reminders that Israel was, and still is, vulnerable from all directions.

In the face of that kind of reality, seeing life as it is, what did they do? They countered with a *Dream!* They dared to believe that they had a corner on the market of the most valuable of all commodities—*the future.* Israel would be the fulcrum on which God would one day move the world. Those audacious Israelites dreamed an impossible dream.

We know what happened. Time after time the cruel events of history shattered that absurd dream. Egypt, Assyria, Persia, Babylonia, Rome all took their turn. But Israel refused to accept the practical lesson of the history of life as it is. Their dream did not dry up like a raisin in the sun. It kept on exploding! Faced with the alternative of abandoning their dreams, and the God who gave them, they chose rather to defer the dream. They learned to wait on the Lord. Today may be dark, and tomorrow may be even blacker, but the day after tomorrow belongs to God!

No civilization has ever lasted very long without a large measure of hope. Century after century the dreamers have dreamed their ancient dreams. But whether from sin, or perversity, or the nature of faith, war and evil have overwhelmed us again and again, and the darkness we thought was but for a night has persisted, despite all the sacrifice and noblest efforts of men to erradicate it. Yet, as long as the dream persisted, history notwithstanding, hope has sustained our human labors and lifted us out of disaster.

America is also a nation and a people founded on a dream, on hope, on the future. Our Declaration of Independence was basically the declaration of a dream. Listen to some of those expressions:

> When in the Course of human events. . . . We hold these truths. . . . created equal . . . unalienable Rights . . . Life, Liberty, and the pursuit of Happiness. . . .

Freedom, equality, opportunity, and justice for all!

Do you remember how Abraham Lincoln put it at Gettysburg?

> Fourscore and seven years ago, our fathers brought forth upon this continent a new nation, conceived in liberty and dedicated to the proposition that all men are created equal.
>
> Now we are engaged in a great civil war, testing whether that nation—or any nation, so conceived and so dedicated—can long endure. . . .

Each successive generation of Americans must keep such dreams alive to show what the destiny of this nation was intended to be from the beginning. And each generation has been ravaged by those whom Mississippi novelist Lillian Smith calls "Killers of the Dream." More than once we have been detoured into the wilderness, into exile, in our search for the Promised Land. Civil War between the states, world wars among the nations, internal disputes, and domestic upheavals have taken their toll.

Today we are almost as disillusioned as Don Quixote and as desperate as ancient Israel. The predictions are not reassuring. Pessimism, skepticism, defeatism, and cynicism are the moods of our day. Too many are old and tried. Too many seem to have grown weary of liberty. Our national agony bothers us. Some consider it to be the last pain in the struggle for life before death comes. But some of us feel that these are the labor pains before the delivery of a new life waiting to be born. And we are tempted to induce labor and get the birth over with. But we don't want to run the risk of a premature birth brought on by the midwifery of what Bonhoeffer called "cheap grace."

The lines adapted from George Bernard Shaw, which Senator Edward Kennedy used at the funeral of his brother Senator Robert Kennedy, are immortal words that will endure:

> Some men see things as they are and ask, Why?
> I dream things that never were and say, Why not?

Into Israel's dark hour of deferred dreams burst Jesus of Nazareth as the custodian of his people's dreams and hopes. He reached into their Scriptures and began to pluck promises that hung there like buds, in the conviction that they were about to burst into full bloom. Dreaming things that never were, he was saying, "Why not? . . . Now!"

A new day was about to dawn. His life was an explosion of hope among a dispirited people. He radiated a powerful new enthusiasm that galvanized his followers. Hope blazed in their breasts. With "majestic instancy" God seemed to be breaking into the world of human events.

There were killers of the dream, though, who were determined to defend their vested interests, determined to keep the status quo, who preferred to have in hand a "raisin in the sun" to an exploding dream, who had learned to live with things as they are and were not too interested in the things that were not yet, that could be. They were satisfied with asking Why? and not dissatisfied enough to say Why not!

Jesus would not dodge reality, nor would he give up his pursuit of what some called an absurd illusion. He knew, centuries before Unamuno said it, that "Only he who attempts the absurd is capable of achieving the impossible."

With shattering candor, Jesus announced to his disciples, "The Son of man must suffer many things, and be rejected . . . and be killed" (Mark 8:31).

Again and again he reminded them that the dream was going to be killed, but that it need not die. Jesus knew the dream was vulnerable, that men could so easily thwart those hopes.

But would that be the end of the affair, would it sag like a heavy load? No! With equal conviction Jesus announced that not even death could defeat and be victor. If disaster was to come with savage swiftness, victory would follow with equal haste. On the one hand, his future was utterly defenseless against tragedy. Soon he would come to the loneliness of the Cross and would cry out, "My God! Why?"

But on the other hand, his future was utterly certain, as triumphant as the promises and power of God. The dream was deferred "for three days" while he went into exile from the land of the living. Then, "in a little while," the dream exploded into a new reality.

During the final decline of the League of Nations, the distinguished Presbyterian preacher-educator Henry Sloane Coffin preached in Washington, D. C. During a walk with Chief Justice of the Supreme Court William Howard Taft, Dr. Coffin asked, "What do you think of the League now?"

Mr. Taft stopped, turned to face Coffin, and said, "You ought to know that in our world the best things get crucified, but they rise again!"

As Christians, we are called to live in that creative tension between the "now" and the "not yet," between things as they are and as they could be, between the actual and the ideal; to sacrifice the securities of the present for the vindication of the future; not only to see things as they are and ask Why?, but to envision things that have never been and say Why not!

Am I another Don Quixote tilting with windmills? I think not. After all, there is nothing much to do but bury a man when the last of his dreams are gone.

The controlling clue to ultimate reality is to be seen in a crucified failure who became a resurrected victor. What we say may fall on apathetic, complacent ears, or be lost in the shouts of a frenzied mob. We may be called upon to endure that desolating loneliness when the truth seems to be buried in a tomb and there is no one to roll away the stone. But that tomb is the emblem of hope. For truth lies like a seed in the soil, soon to burst forth and bear fruit. The tomb in which men try to bury truth becomes the womb in which fresh new wisdom is born that will outlive its pallbearers.

The man of hope is frequently gripped by a feeling of helplessness as he watches those who use crude, blunt instruments of power to bludgeon his most cherished convictions to death. He is easily tempted to leap into the fray and fight with his enemies' weapons rather than to work for the vindication of God. Jesus dared to believe that a dream deferred is not a dream destroyed. It is

> not "like a raisin in the sun,"
>> not "a festering sore,"
>>> not "a heavy load that sags."

It is something that "explodes!"

Man of La Mancha climaxes with Don Quixote dying. He cannot remember anything of his past. Aldonza comes in and says, "You are my lord, Don Quixote."

But he cannot remember. She says, "Everything. My whole life. You spoke to me and everything was different! You looked at me and called me by another name! Dulcinea . . . Dulcinea. . . . When you spoke her name an angel seemed to whisper. . . . Won't you please bring back the dream of Dulcinea? . . . Won't you bring me the bright and shining glory of Dulcinea?"

Quixote stirs a bit and says, "Perhaps, perhaps . . . it was not a dream."

Then Aldonza begins to speak softly,

"To dream the impossible dream. . . .
To fight the unbeatable foe. . . .
To bear with unbearable sorrow. . . .
To run where the brave dare not go. . . . "

And Quixote, remembering, sings,

"To right the unrightable wrong. . . .
To try when your arms are too weary. . . .
To reach the unreachable star!"

A dream, too long deferred, had exploded in one woman. Aldonza the prostitute was seen as Dulcinea the lady fair. And she came to believe that's what she could be— a lady.

This is what Jesus did for people. He dared to believe that a dream deferred is not a dream destroyed. He dreamed impossible dreams about people, and some of them believed and became children of God.

> Jesus looked up and said to her, "Woman, where are they? Has no one condemned you?"
>
> She said, "No one, Lord."
>
> And Jesus said, "Neither do I condemn you; go, and do not sin again."
>
> But to all who received him, who believed in his name, he gave power to become children of God. . . .
> —John 8:10-11; 1:12